Taken to the Edge of Insanity.
My Survival Unexpected.
This is my story.

I MARRIED A
SOCIOPATH

Sabrina Brown, DrPH

I MARRIED A SOCIOPATH

This book is dedicated to

Paul and Anne Vincent,

Damon and Lisa Viele,

and my endlessly supportive husband, Steven.

A Note to the Readers

I STARTED BLOGGING IN FEBRUARY of 2012. I made a decision to take my journaling on-line, making my story available to others, but under the protection of an alias. Portions of this book come from "stand alone" posts from my blog. They may appear out of place amidst my storyline, but I feel like the message within them is important enough to leave them as is. Posts at various time periods reveal my thoughts and feelings at that time, which may or may not be where or who I am today. By capturing emotions in "real time" I hope others can better relate to surviving the same sort of adversities. The events that I've chosen to document in this book are the ones that have been the most painful and/or had the greatest effect on me. Some events may seem trivial in comparison to others, but will come to fruition in book two and three—the seeds were planted within the timeline of this book.

The process from blog to book, under my real identity, has been agonizingly difficult—an unexpected internal struggle. It has taken five years to not only write my book, but to find the courage to uncover and claim myself. Fear has gotten in the way of so much and fear has kept me imprisoned. My transformation to living freely is manifesting, in part, with the publication of my story.

—Sabrina Brown, DrPH

"Where I am and who I am is the totality of where I've been and who I was. Those in my past do not know me, though; I am not there anymore. But there will always be those who judge me from where we parted, not looking for where I am in the distance."

I MARRIED A SOCIOPATH

1 HOW I CAME TO BE

WE WERE PLAYING, MY BROTHER and I, at our favorite spot in the nearby creek, under the bridge, and then, he was just there. He overcame me without hesitation and flung me down on a big rock like a rag doll. I knew what was coming next and yelled, over and over, for my brother to not look and to run home. The piercing pain overwhelmed me; I was being ripped in half. My little nine-year-old body hit the rock again and again, wounding me everywhere. He was so heavy that I couldn't breathe, and I was so cold. Then, he was gone as fast as he had appeared. I slid into the cold water. I lost time. When I stood, I could see blood running down my shin. I don't remember putting my overalls back on. It was dark by the time I staggered home. My mind could not process why my favorite uncle would do this, so the memory slid down into a dark forgotten place, but not without effect.

Three years later, that same uncle gave me a brand new Darcy Barbie Doll. She had a house and clothes. I played with her all day. I was so happy. Then he lay down on the floor beside me and said, "Don't you know you are the ugly one? These aren't for you. These are for my beautiful daughter, who looks like a Barbie Doll." And he took them from me to give to her. I believed what he said down to the nucleus of every cell, because this is how we adopt shame, we don't feel the ugliness simply in something specific, like our faces, it defines every minute part of us, individually and altogether; it's inescapable.

· · · · ·

My mother was one of five children; they lived in extreme poverty. There were four boys; she had three older brothers, and one younger brother. The oldest brother lived far away so we didn't interact much, but when his wife divorced him, she was ostracized by the rest of the family. I heard the whisperings. The two middle brothers and their wives would meet at the local Perkins to discuss how to handle the family secrets, of which my mother had been a big part her whole life. Despite this complicity, my mother and I have a beautiful story of forgiveness. I believe that she was abused; overall, it's likely that she endured more than I did. I learned to love her within the context of her life story, though she has not shared very much with me, what she has, is absolutely heartbreaking. I believe, now, looking back, that she sometimes dissociated during my childhood, particularly after something happened to me, being triggered herself.

. . . . .

The youngest brother was "my favorite uncle" because I was told this as truth at a very young age. This is the uncle who had hurt me and had taken the Darcy doll from me. I remember being pulled from school and taken to court to testify about his being my favorite uncle, against his ex-wife, so that he could gain some custody of his daughter. The family had united to take down this "terrible" woman. The reality is that my uncle was a known drug addict, had committed armed robbery and spent time in Attica, which is why he lost custody of his daughter. He was ultimately awarded supervised visitations. Generally, my parents or grandparents supervised. I was taken to visit him while he was in prison. I was encouraged to write to him. Later, as an adult, I apologized to my aunt. I loved her. As a child, I hadn't known what I was doing. She told me of his abuse, which was nothing less than torture. One example is that he would straddle her while she was face up and tap on her chest bone, hard, repeatedly, and just look at her, for hours.

He married again. When his second wife divorced him, the family turned against her, too. She also told me of his torture. I use the word torture because it is not impulsive or inconsistent domestic violence that is later regretted. It is systematic, *controlled*, thoughtful abuse designed to break down a victim, designed to control her.

She told me that this favorite uncle of mine watched his father, my grandfather, molest young girls from the church where he pastored. He was jealous that they got so much attention, so he learned to hate little girls and women, overall. She told me she was thankful they had not had a daughter.

. . . . .

When I was fifteen, that uncle took me on a motorcycle ride to what seemed like an auto mechanic's shop. There, we met up with a friend of his. This is where I had my turn at being tortured. I endured approximately thirteen hours at their hands.

He was high, his friend was high. They blindfolded me. The other man came in and touched me first, then hit me. Hard. They threw me on the ground and, then it began. I spat on them and screamed. One held me down and the other put something inside me to open me up. They then took an apple and put it inside me, pulled out the other object, pushed my legs together and tied them tight. Putting my legs together like that—it felt like the pain of natural childbirth. I wailed in agony. I stayed in that pain, not knowing when or if it would end (unlike the pain of childbirth). I thought I was going to die. I screamed a gut wrenching, horrible, scream... then I detached from reality. When they took the apple out, I spat on them, again. I screamed that I would not be broken. That's when my uncle put a plastic bag over my head. I couldn't breathe; I thought I would die. I let go of everything that mattered for just one

4

more breath. I was gasping… then I passed out. When I woke up, they had removed the bag, but immediately put it back on. More gasping, more panic. I slowed my breathing and, this time, I wanted to die. I passed out. When I woke up again, the bag was off. I screamed, "No! I'm alive! No! I don't want to wake up! No! I want to die! Please, no more! Let me die… no… more…" The bag went back on. I woke for a third time under a tree, naked and cold. My uncle approached me and he was carrying a shovel; he thought I was dead. When he saw that I wasn't, he kicked me. He told me to get dressed, threw my clothes on me and then threw me into the back of a truck.

. . . . .

Two years prior to the rape on the rock by the creek, I found myself in the shed behind my grandparents' home. My grandfather had started molesting me when I was a toddler, me and several of my cousins. We told our parents what was happening; one of my cousins even showed her father what grandpa would do, so the family had found him out, but, as it often goes in these cases, especially when the complicit party is of the previous generation, nothing was done. So, his behavior escalated, as do the actions of most abusers. They test to determine what they can get away with and they escalate, test and escalate…

His hands were wrapped around my neck and his fingers pressed into the front of my throat. I was face down on a dirty wooden table, bent over, and I felt like a sword was entering my bottom. He stopped and threw me down on the dirt floor; he urinated on me while telling me, all the while, what a worthless little girl I was. I felt like I needed to poop, so I went to the bathroom in the house. I don't remember how I got there. I locked the door, then stood in the dry shower. I looked down and could see the little splatters of blood hit the tile. I went to the toilet, thinking still that I had to poop, then back to the shower. Though the bathroom was already filthy (my grandparents lived in filth), I was afraid of the mess that I had made on the floor. I used a washcloth to clean the floor, then the toilet, then the entire room.

My cousin came to the window of my grandparents' bathroom, wondering where I had been, and she saw me trying to hang myself from the door. She screamed and banged on the window. I was in a lost state of mind and slowly I became aware of the present and saw her. She looked afraid. I took the towel off of my neck, went over to the window and opened it. She asked why I was still in the bathroom. I said that I couldn't stop feeling like I had to go to the bathroom.

She left and came back with flowers, white lilies of the valley. She hand-picked them and they smelled so good. I pressed them to my face and the horrible smells enveloping me dissipated. She and I always comforted each other the best that we could, knowing, but not *really* knowing, what was happening to us. Lily of the valley flowers are both delicate and dangerous. Like this complex flower, childhood attacks made me both fragile and violent. Little did I know, the worst was yet to come.

. . . . .

When my parents returned to pick me up, my grandmother went on and on about how I had cleaned the bathroom, saying, "she was in there all day." The worst and most confusing part is that I was forced to act as though nothing had happened. My grandfather, having suffered a stroke, was not held accountable for anything, especially by the second oldest brother, "if he was even capable," because, "his mind wasn't clear." At picnics, per his request, my place was set next to his. I hated when he bent over to give me a goodbye kiss: all I remember is a lot of slobber and stubble, and feeling sick.

2

THE SOCIOPATH AND CONTROL—THERE

FROM THE BEGINNING

I MET PETER WHEN I was fifteen years old at summer camp. I believed that he was my knight in shining armor and that he was going to take me away from this horror story. He was the best looking boy I had ever met; he was Canadian (which, in my adolescence, made him a little mysterious), classy and downright *perfect*. We connected immediately, realizing that we had also gone to the same camp as children. His dad, John Walton, pastored the largest church in our denomination. Peter and his brother, aided by their very well-known last name, were the most romantically sought-after boys in this small community of faith.

I fell head-over-heels for Peter. He was shy and happy to be pursued. He had a certain intensity about him, and was very interested in everything that I did. I couldn't believe that someone like him was attracted to someone like me.

Looking back, I see that I bore a close resemblance to *Anne of Green Gables*, and was called this endearingly by my high school music teacher, but I thought of myself more like *Pippi Longstocking*: disheveled, ill-mannered and unwelcome. Whereas Anne was well kept, orderly and disciplined, Pipi lived by her own rules and was judged harshly. I longed to be as free, confident, fearless, outspoken and strong as Pippi, my heroine. I read those books over and over, trying to escape self-loathing. I hated everything about myself. I couldn't ever get "clean." I was completely different than all of the other girls, both inside and out. I was ashamed to shower in the gym locker room, change for swimming practice. I had never seen anyone like me—pale and freckled with red hair. Redheads were not considered attractive when I grew up; *Pretty Woman* was years away. Peter was so handsome and I was so flattered that he was drawn to me.

To impress Peter, I started to borrow clothes from my best friend, Cassie. I was a "redneck" and he was from an "important" family, so I needed to portray perfection. We dated off-and-on until I left for college, four hundred miles away. It is important to note the "on again, off again" nature of our relationship. Peter broke up with me often and without reason, in order to unsettle me and maintain control. He even broke up with me after my high school graduation party; at graduation I received numerous awards and a lot of attention, which otherwise would have bolstered my confidence. As soon as I began to move on and regain confidence, he showed up, literally, on my doorstep. He pursued me to the exact level of my detachment from him, never more.

. . . . .

When Peter arrived on my college campus in my second year, giving up a Division I baseball scholarship to do so, I was informally dating someone else from a nearby university. Thinking back, this other relationship was a normal one that might have evolved into something serious. During the time of freedom before Peter arrived, I had three roommates, two of whom are still dear friends. My roommates and I talked often about the future and tried to predict where we would each end up. I was so ambitious and career-oriented; I earned my Federal Communications Commission license before I obtained my driver's license, and had been a weekend Disk Jockey at a local radio station by my junior year in high school. We all joked that I would not have children, if I ever even got married. I wanted to be a national news anchor.

. . . . .

I should have seen what was coming. The first thing Peter demanded was that I throw away all of my makeup. He had given up a lot, so I listened and obeyed. I thought that I looked uglier, unable to hide my pale skin and freckles. I lost my newfound confidence and independence, along with all of my male friends and most of my female friends.

As a freshman, Peter played second-string catcher. Out-of-season practices were early morning and afternoon, and sometimes the team was back to the gym practicing as late as midnight. He dreaded the actual season. To me everything seemed to be falling into place for him, perfectly; a pitcher had been drafted to the minor leagues, so there was hope of him also being drafted. One evening, Peter came into my room and announced that he had quit. The coach was harsh, the practices were too intense, and combined with college-level academics, it was too much for him. I tried to convince him to go back; I really liked watching him play and I dreamed of him going pro, so his departure was a blow to me, too. Looking back, there is no way that he could have sustained through the rigor of the program. There was too much work and not nearly enough praise. He failed academically that first semester, but his father did what he did best—swooped in, saving Peter from any consequence, and brought his son back to the college where *he* had influence, where Peter could start afresh.

. . . . .

Peter and I had started having sex the previous Christmas. By Easter, I started to experience symptoms much like mononucleosis (which I thought I had) and vomited regularly. Peter said that he would visit, and when he did, we got a hotel room. He suggested that we buy a pregnancy test. When I saw the positive result, I became hysterical, though he was strangely calm and accepting.

A short time later, he came to visit me, and in the car, he told me that he had had sex with a girl several times while visiting Canada. He was my first, my only, but I was not "his first" as he had professed. I jumped out of the moving vehicle and ran down the road in two feet of snow. I had zero coping skills. I was now trapped with a baby, no alternatives and the realization that our relationship was a mirage. And there were other girls. I knew it in my gut, but he so earnestly defended himself that I believed him.

. . . . .

Hiding a pregnancy at a conservative college is excruciatingly lonely. I had been elected to homecoming court my freshman year being popular for the first time in my entire life. Then, suddenly, I was throwing up in a dorm room bathroom and only my roommates knew what was going on. While I was barely able to keep any food down, simply trying to get through the semester, Peter re-engaged with a former girlfriend, which he did not reveal to me until our honeymoon.

Enjoying my newfound freedom, before finding out I was pregnant, I had planned to stay over the summer and not return home; I had already acquired a salaried job as an admission counselor and, as part of my program, an additional part time job at the campus radio station. I was easily able to support myself. Peter insisted I move to where he had transferred instead of him moving back to me. I had the more stable established situation, was set to graduate early and loved my college, my broadcast journalism degree program and friends, but he was convincing and I was afraid to be alone and pregnant. I was afraid he would break up with me if I didn't go with his plan. By the end of the semester, I gave up the jobs. I transferred to Peter's school; back to his home, not mine. This was a notable mistake—I could've made it on my own—I had support in that little community. I should've stayed. My family came to pick me up. I was so stressed that I didn't realize until hours into the trip that I had forgotten all of my clothes.

. . . . .

Telling my father, the most important person in my life, that I was pregnant was really hard. A girl who had never even been to the principal's office, one that had made him so proud, now only offered disappointment. He did a fantastic job of making me feel loved. He handled it as well as he could, paid for a shotgun wedding and became supportive of the child to come. I went into labor at his home; he was downright excited by then. My daughter loved her Papa.

. . . . .

On our honeymoon, Peter told me about more women. It was anything but romantic. I was nineteen, almost five months pregnant, and in a remote cabin in the Adirondack Mountains. Had I known about his many exploits prior to marriage, I would have not married him. Had I known earlier, I would have had the resources and support to help me process what I was hearing, and to make a more rational decision. I had given myself over and I had trusted him, and he had simply done what he wanted.

I was isolated in a time before cell phones or internet, in a place that barely had electricity. Everything that I had believed was shattered. I was alone with a man I no longer knew and I panicked. I had become a strong, ambitious, driven girl, and now I was vulnerable and imprisoned. Wanting to get away, both physically and emotionally, I ran out of the cabin in my underwear. It had rained the entire week, so it was very muddy. As I ran I fell, got up and kept running. He came after me. I was crying and falling. He finally caught up with me, grabbed me and dragged me back to the cabin. He had no sympathy for me and forced me to stay the rest of the time.

I didn't know how to handle all of the lies and deceit and the situation I found myself. I was married and pregnant; I believed I had no way out. This is exactly why he waited to tell me. He waited until I was trapped and isolated before he told me things that could have provided the last push that I needed to extract myself from the relationship.

This event was the start of Peter documenting my mental illness. It was also just the beginning of Peter systematically detailing to me intimacies that he had experienced with other women, but had withheld from me. He enjoyed withholding from me, while placating me, telling me that he was capable of being a good and loving husband if only I could be more perfect, more of what *he* desired. Our relationship was never about who I was, only who he wanted me to be. In my sheltered, naïve, nineteen-year-old, *hormonal* mind, my hopes and dreams of love and romance were crushed that day in the mountains.

. . . . .

This event appeared in a custody dispute court motion, against me, twenty years later, but was written quite differently than my recount. In this other version, I just "went crazy" for no reason at all. The times and dates of an endless string of events during which I just "went crazy" filled hundreds of his journal pages—all distorted reality. He had a shoebox full of written ammunition, and he had waited for the perfect time to fire.

3 ISOLATION

I TOOK A SEMESTER OFF from college to care for my newborn daughter while Peter continued taking classes. One girl from Peter's honeymoon confessions was in an evening class of his. I was dealing with hormones, exhaustion and isolation, and trying to come to terms with a post-pregnancy body at twenty years old. Peter shared his struggles with fantasizing about the girl in class and, thereby, coerced me into having sex less than two weeks after a vaginal birth to an eight-pound baby. The doctor-recommended interim between giving birth and having intercourse is six weeks. It was very painful and likely the reason that I later ended up back in the hospital. I lived to please him. I feared that he would have sex with the girl from his evening class. I adapted to this fear without consideration for myself.

Married life was awful. I worked at a daycare and took only two week's maternity leave after my daughter was born. I ended up back in the hospital with an infection; the doctors stated that I had not taken enough time to rest. Leaving college to have a baby at twenty is hard. Moving across the road from my new husband's parents was downright foolish. Life resembled the show *Everybody Loves Raymond*, but without humor. My in-laws constantly judged me. Peter never saw anything wrong with the way they behaved, insisting that it was all in my head. His mother often reminded me that I had ruined her son's life. My in-laws referred to me as "the seductress" behind my back. I was right where Peter wanted me.

Peter's dad's prominence in the denomination turned us into celebrities because of the scandal of pregnancy. We were young, poor, isolated and overwhelmed, trying to act the opposite. I was rarely spoken to because of my figurative scarlet letter; I missed my former roommates from college. Every week we were required to attend Sunday church, followed by lunch at the Walton's. I felt incredibly tense around John and Elaine, Peter's mother. If Peter wasn't around, they entirely ignored me.

Only one person mattered: my daughter. She was beautiful, and became the center of everyone's attention. Often, she wasn't in the nursery when I went to pick her up after church. Peter's mother would pick her up early in order to pass her around in the foyer of the church. My daughter cried a lot on Sundays, perhaps from being handled by so many people.

My in-laws sometimes invited another family or two over for lunch after church. For these lunches, Elaine started the meal the day before and worked for hours after returning home from church. John arrived later than everyone else, in an obvious euphoric state from the attention. He asked Elaine about his sermon, expecting only accolades. If she offered even a slight criticism, rage flashed across his face. Peter continually told me over the years that his father was more emotionally available from "the mound" (the pulpit) than he ever was at home. That's when he felt closest to John. Because of this and because of his father's constant traveling and Peter being overall neglected, I wondered in those early years if Peter had an attachment disorder that prevented intimacy.

I don't recall Peter's dad looking at his mother with anything other than disgust. If she spoke, sometimes about characters in the romance novels she was reading, he quickly dismissed her. She embarrassed the family. It was painfully obvious that all of the male Waltons were disgusted with the family's matriarch. Now I realize that I was observing misogyny.

Figure one is a flowchart showing the dynamic I observed between Walton men and their female partners.

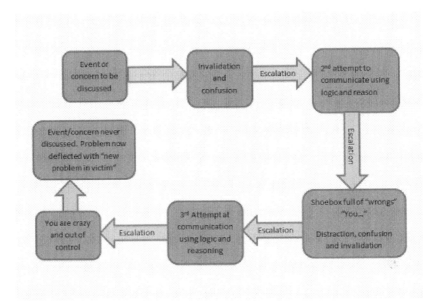

Figure one also illustrates the cycle between Peter and me when there was conflict. The only difference between John and Elaine and Peter and me is that sometimes there was just only one level of escalation before Elaine's immediate submission. Elaine submitted over and over again, and endured continual verbal abuse. The consequence of her response, in contrast to mine (increased emotional escalation), manifested itself in physical ailments. She was severely depressed and plagued by arthritis. She had several surgeries (five, I believe, within the twenty four years that I knew her) and seemed unhealthy, overall. John commented on her lack of physical health and gave her positive attention when she was ill. She did not seem to do anything for herself—excepting excessive spending for/gift giving to others—and hardly bought a thing for herself. She was in constant pain, taking pain medications, and had migraines for days at a time.

I always felt compassion for Elaine, believing her to be in a tough spot. She gave up her education to support John and then gave up her health for him and their three sons.

. . . . .

Part of a pastor's job is to counsel families within the church community. After lunches, Peter's family discussed church parishioners; these discussions included private details that John learned through counseling. I heard about a woman who had undergone an abortion before getting married, and had not told her new husband. I heard of the CEO of a major corporation who had confided in his pastor that his son had molested his daughter for their entire youth. The daughter, then a grown woman, was divorcing because of sexual problems, and her husband had threatened to expose the family secret. The local physician had been having an affair with his secretary for decades, and his wife had just found out; he and his mistress had attempted suicide.

I felt uncomfortable around the congregation on Sundays. I should not have known their secrets. Not only was confidence broken, their misfortunes were also critiqued and analyzed. In time, I learned that I, too, was being discussed, critiqued, and analyzed. I was frustrated for most of my marriage by the stern judgments and hypocrisies that came from the Waltons, all under the guise of religiosity.

My only outlet was church activities. If I started to connect, even at church, I was discouraged, by Peter, with silence and withholding. A sociopath can never be pleased, though I tried with all my might. The faux camaraderie only emerges after complete submission to their needs. I still shudder, thinking about Peter's expectations and about what I gave up for so long. Even the slightest attachment or connection made to someone other than him was met with a dark, empty coldness, difficult to describe.

. . . . .

Within a few years of the marriage, I started having nightmares, and began to struggle with distinguishing reality from my dreams. My mind was not able to handle the constant strain of contradiction. Peter suggested that I see a therapist, recommended by his father. It was his father's therapist, and John thought that she was the best person to handle my "mental illness." The whole family became involved in helping me. I was a distraction from the real problem: John. I later learned of the deep-seated family secret, his sexual deviance and misogyny. In order to perpetuate a secret, distraction is requisite. I was the "identified patient."

4 THE EXORCISM

RIGHT ACROSS THE STREET from the church and our apartment, sat my grandparents' old house. Being so near was more than difficult. Peter knew about my past, but didn't understand that seeing that house was like scratching a scab just as it was about to heal. I had to start all over again. This fresh-again wound and the fact that nothing had prepared me for real life—to be a mother and wife, and bear financial responsibility, all within a hostile, unloving environment—made the everyday of living so lonely. Good parenting is difficult when you have a loving partner. Their logic was that I must have had a demon in me. No one would behave the way that I did unless they were possessed.

Peter was completing his undergraduate degree in religion and history, and working as a janitor at his father's church. I studied while working and taking care of my baby. Peter studied at the library with "study partners."

I was still having nightmares and trouble distinguishing between reality and dream life. Peter and his family said that my abusive past was manifesting in my adult life, destroying *him*. My family was a problem, I was a problem, just like the parishioners in the church were a problem. I was under a microscope, being analyzed and judged. I was getting worse and becoming more of a nuisance. They needed to identify the problem, extract it from the family, and show that they played a part in this resolution. Peter met a fellow religion student who was familiar with exorcisms. After they determined that I was possessed, Peter and I went on a retreat.

At the retreat, I was assessed. Yes, I was definitely possessed. I sat with the man in charge of the retreat house, he laid his hands on my forehead and began to speak in tongues. It was impressive; it sounded like another language. He pushed me and it was over. We were asked to stay in the house to make sure the demons did not re-emerge. After the weekend, we went home. I was terrified. My nightmares became more vivid and I began hallucinating. The exorcist came to us this time. We went to John's office because he offered and seemed to enjoy participating in sensational matters. He again laid hands on me and spoke in tongues. I was healed this time with no more demons.

At this point, the Walton family asserted that I was not only mentally ill, but also spiritually evil, and definitely unfit to mother my daughter. I was exhausted, lonely, isolated, confused, young, naïve and married to a sociopath, who was incapable of true warmth. Still, I went along with Peter's "suggestions," so as not to lose any of his attention. Going along with his suggestions was the only time that he showed kindness and concern for me.

. . . . .

Early in John's career, his work required a lot of travel. Growing up, Peter moved every two-to-five years. John would settle into a new job; the family, into new schools, activities and friends, trying to establish a community. Then, John would find a better job or need to leave for reasons he failed to identify. Peter later speculated this was likely due to affairs that would have affected his job and/or reputation if he stayed.

In the years I knew John Walton, I observed his disquiet, discontent, and lack of concern for anyone else, unless it benefited him in some way. He demanded center stage and relentless praise, and would become agitated or downright aggressive without it. John Walton bought homes above his means and then borrowed money from the church, relatives or friends, or he rented an apartment within the home and scaled down for a while. The family would move down the street, across town, or to another city or country. All moves required new decor, window treatments, rugs and fixtures—always the best, and usually on credit. John Walton dressed impeccably, in line with the latest fashion, right down to eyewear. I never thought that any of the Walton men were financially sound. Though they prayed before every meal and quoted Scripture often, especially when at odds with their latest enemy, it felt superficial and empty to be around them. Their interactions lacked love, empathy and intimacy.

. . . . .

While finishing college, I worked again at the local radio station where I began my journalism career as a junior in high school. My first newscast was at 6:00 a.m., which meant that I was on the road by 4:30 a.m. This schedule allowed me to be back home to watch my daughter by 2:30 p.m.

When I graduated from college, Peter decided our apartment was too small to accommodate a toddler, so we moved in with John and Elaine. After six months of a very uncomfortable existence (my early mornings for example), John announced that he and Elaine were moving back to Canada. Us living with them was not easy for anyone, which could have been the reason or they may have been avoiding a problem or relationship in the church. They told us only that they were moving, which meant that we were moving, and not returning to the church where John pastored.

We abruptly moved to a little town about twenty miles down the road, so that Peter could quit his job and pursue a graduate degree in history. I continued work at the local radio station. This was our third move and second church within our two years of marriage.

The first heating bill of the winter was approximately three hundred dollars; we couldn't make ends meet. Peter decided to take a semester off and start a modeling career. He spent nearly one thousand dollars paying fees and having professional headshots taken. Meanwhile, I went to the local health department and received Women Infants and Children (WIC) support and food stamps, and tried to get heating help. It wasn't enough; though Peter was making money, it was not steady money.

I got a new job at a better radio station in public radio. There, as a reporter, I covered a high-profile court trial. It was then that I met the lead reporter for the largest radio station in the area. He introduced me to the news director, who started to mentor me. I didn't have quite enough experience, but I had potential, and they had an open reporter position. I didn't get the position, but started in a different overnight position—a seemingly backward move, but this station was a flagship of the East Coast.

After a few months, I worked my way up to reporter and weekend news anchor. I loved what I did, and I was good at it. My self-confidence and self-worth were budding. The promotions and prestige, combined with the attention from the news director and my boss, helped me to feel attractive for the first time in my life. I confided in Peter about my boss—he was flirtatious and it made me feel special. I guess I did this to point out that not everyone thought I was ugly, like he did. That admission was a mistake and he used it against me for our entire marriage. My success was also a problem.

Shortly thereafter, I became pregnant with my second child. During those weekend hours, I was vomiting before the top and bottom of the newscasts. The promise of a newfound career came to a screeching halt, and so did the attention that I had grown to crave. At five months pregnant, I was a liability reporting on the street. I was again given a morning newscaster position, on a sister station, where I was up at 4:30 a.m. for a 6:00 a.m. start. This meant I was out of the main newsroom, sitting at a soundboard, by myself, for the entire shift. They only kept me part-time. We still could not make ends meet.

One morning, as I drove to work at 4:30 a.m., the roads had not yet been plowed, I ran out of gas. I had to walk nearly a mile to the closest gas station with spare change that I found on the car floor; I was crying by the time I got there. The young man at the counter paid for a few dollars of gas so that I could get to the station on time. I delivered my first newscast and then lost it, sobbing in front of the entire morning crew. I didn't know how I would get home. Later that day, the local male radio celebrity gave me ten dollars for gas. He then asked me if I had anything for lunch—I rarely did—and he gave me another ten dollars. There was a food court on the first floor; during my lunch break, I nearly ran downstairs. I ate for the entire half hour. Periodically, during my pregnancy, I would find five-dollar bills on the radio board where I delivered my newscasts.

Peter took no responsibility for providing for his family. While I was waiting for him to pick me up one day, a homeless man approached me and asked for money. He said that he was starving. I looked at him and said, "so am I." In that moment, I realized that I was always hungry. There is almost nothing worse than wondering if and when you'll eat again.

5 FROM ON-AIR TO DESPAIR

I DECIDED THAT I HAD to find an additional job. I interviewed at a local television station for a weekend producer position. The news director took one look at my belly and said, "What are we going to do about a maternity leave?" Being desperate, I bargained that if he gave me the job, I would only take two weeks off. Based on my qualifications, he agreed.

I was working from 4:30 a.m. until 1:30 p.m., then going home to watch my three-year-old. Saturdays and Sundays were usually ten-hour days, unless breaking news called me in earlier. The 11:00 p.m. news kept me at the station until midnight and if a show or game ran late, then it was later.

. . . . .

I gave birth to my second daughter naturally, under Peter's advisement that I not damage the children during childbirth. I do not believe that the health of our children was his motivation for having me suffer.

One evening right before the 6:00 p.m. news, I had to pump (I was breastfeeding) and there was so much, because I had gone all day, that it was taking more than the usual fifteen minutes. The news anchor started paging me over the loudspeaker, so I came out of the bathroom holding up baggies for the newsroom to see, and asked that he give me a break. No one working in the newsroom had a child, most were near thirty and I was twenty three with two children. I was chastised for not being available and my job was threatened.

When my second daughter was four months old, the weekend anchor left for a job with CNN. I—the ideal candidate, considering my experience producing—who could do two jobs and be paid for one, was asked to train for the position. Weeks after my training began, Peter announced that, as he was praying, the Lord told him to go to seminary in Kentucky. We visited the campus and I began to hunt for a house and a job. I found a townhome with rent based on income. I landed a highly-competitive full-time job at a local television station. I had made the jump to on-air talent. I agreed to help produce, as it paid more than the reporter position. We packed and moved to Kentucky where Peter started a theology degree.

We arrived on a Wednesday and I started work that Friday. The first day of work, in a new city, there was a breaking news story of twin boys who had accidentally locked themselves in an old refrigerator—the kind that cannot be opened from the inside. They had suffocated and died. I covered the parents, which meant we needed to get what the television industry calls B-roll (the video to fill the voiceover parts of the story). The home was over two hours away. Another reporter and a camera man went with me. While we were attempting to get B-roll, the father pulled out a rifle and aimed it at the news vehicle. The other reporter jumped behind the wheel and the cameraman threw his camera into the back of the vehicle, then dove in through the window—a live shot for the *Eleven O'clock News*, and then teardown. The drive back got me home at 3:00 a.m. This is the nature of journalism; if it's a big story, you work around the clock. I was given a clothing allowance and salon services, and, as a breaking news reporter, I was starting to get recognized while out in public. Peter was not happy with the freedom, independence and public recognition that I was receiving. And he was not happy that I was working with men.

Within a few months, I was asked to fill in for a noon newscast anchor. Following that, the news director had me read the first ten minutes of the newscast after the *Eleven O'clock News*; I was being groomed for an anchor position, learning the journalism ropes and becoming more successful. As my success at work grew, our home continued to deteriorate, despite the fact that we were finally making ends meet for the first time.

Things are almost always tense in a newsroom leading up to a newscast. One Sunday night, when I was producing an eleven o'clock newscast, I accidentally typed "Whore" into the tele-prompter several times for the sportscaster whose name rhymed with the word. The directing staff thought it was hilarious, and the harder we laughed, the angrier the sports anchor became. During a commercial break, he threw down his lapel microphone and stormed into the director's booth. He was screaming at us while we were in tears from fits of laughter. Yelling is also typical in journalism, so it didn't faze us. After the newscast, he and I were the only ones left in the building. He cornered me and started yelling again. I thought he was going to start swinging, so I ducked under his arm and ran out of the building to my car. He was chasing after me, still yelling. He realized that he had crossed the line and, by the time he was backpedaling, it was too late, I was already scared.

When I got home, I was upset and didn't want to get out of bed the next day. Peter took this single opportunity to begin extracting me from this career once and for all. As always, I agreed to his "suggestions." He drove me to a facility for the mentally ill and signed me over. He claimed that I had tried to kill myself with some prescription sleeping medication; I was put on suicide watch for three days. I had not tried to kill myself with sleeping medication, but I agreed because I did think I needed help… or maybe just some sleep.

When I got out, I was required to attend another week of outpatient services. The news director was more-than-willing to work with me, which was surprising, because this sort of event is often seen as scandalous for a "local celebrity." I was finding my independence away from Peter, identifying my talents and developing a promising career. Most importantly, self-efficacy was taking root. Killing this sense of self-reliance is fundamental to maintaining control in a relationship. Despite the station's support, Peter convinced me that I could no longer handle the rigors of being a television journalist. He insisted that I stay at home with the girls and assured me that he would get a job and go to school part-time.

I quit and stayed at home. No one believed that I would quit a job where two hundred applicants were waiting to replace me. It took me a decade to build a career that I loved—landed my dream job with a promising future—and just days for Peter to tear it down.

In 1977, Albert Bandera published a seminal paper defining self-efficacy as: *"...A person's belief that they can succeed in situations* [1]." Weak self-efficacy means a person would avoid challenges; believing anything that's challenging to be beyond their individual capabilities, a focus on failings and negative outcomes, and diminished confidence in personal abilities. An abuser does not want their victim thinking they have any options but to stay and tolerate however they're forced to live. The victim begins to circle around the abuser, losing mindfulness of self and purpose, thinking everything is beyond their control. The sociopath feeds on this weakness, gaining power and control. Just a few years out of college, I was weak and helpless.

. . . . .

Peter believed that I was so unstable that he needed to help by earning a counseling degree. He worked at a religious home for troubled children who were removed from their homes for various behavioral problems. Peter worked evenings and most weekends, so he could study and take classes during the week at the seminary. When he wasn't working, he needed a lot of time and quiet, even needing to stay in a hotel during stressful times in the semester.

Evenings and weekends are generally family time, and the city that we lived in had very few social activities—no McDonalds, no public library, no central place to meet people. Additionally, I had given up good full-time pay, Peter was making minimum wage and with seminary being very expensive; we had very little to live on, despite having moved in order to help our finances. For me, rural life on a tight budget was a recipe for near-complete isolation with limited options.

After six months of staying at home, I genuinely almost lost my mind. My fast-paced, highly competitive, somewhat glamorous job had vanished in a flash, and I had been cut off from my colleagues, the only people I knew. I was without a car most days, had limited financial resources, and was caring for two toddlers. I didn't know what to do with my time and combined with all of the medications I was prescribed after being hospitalized, most days I acted more like a zombie than a human being.

A female director with whom I had worked was the only colleague who kept in touch with me. She had disposable money; I was vulnerable and lonely, craving connection, ready to accept attention from anyone—and she was paying. I had a scavenger mentality. I didn't want a sexual relationship, I had lost my sex drive with the first rounds of nausea and learning I was pregnant. What I did want was some help with logistics—transportation for the girls, some meals out, some freedom—friendship and emotional support. I was willing to trade sexual acts for these things—that's what she was asking.

My relationship with this former director lasted one month. This all damaged me further. I was ashamed of myself. This was the first time I ever crossed the line in my marriage—Peter and I had been married for three years. The little self-esteem that I had gained from my ten year journalism career, plummeted to new depths. Peter revealed to me, years later, that he actually welcomed my infidelities because it allowed him "permission" to do whatever he pleased. He used this first indiscretion as evidence of my severe mental illness and had me admitted into an outpatient program, this time for a month. Professionals there agreed with Peter that the relationship was a sign of mental illness; my male psychiatrist asked little more than the details of the encounters. Peter used all of this against me during our divorce proceedings and to poison my daughters against me.

The whole Walton family was homophobic and they expressed this openly and often. I believe that Peter's reaction to my affair was a projection onto me of his own issues. He had homosexual tendencies, and told me of fantasies he had about male friends of his. During my treatment, Peter called phone sex lines, racking up hundreds of dollars in charges.

. . . . .

I remember needing milk for the girls, then one and four years old, and having no car, no family nearby and no friends, I decided to put the girls in their wagon and walked to the store. It was approaching ninety degrees outside, it was a hilly route and it was nearly a three mile walk, one way. Peter was working a double shift and would not be home until the next day. I made this trek often, even in the cold of the winter and the heat of the summer. I was alone with the girls nearly all day, most days, sometimes with no money for food. Again, I applied for food stamps and WIC. I also began to "wheel" the girls to the local food bank across town.

I love my children more than anything and I was doing my best for them. Peter was usually a passive parent, but doled out harsh corporal punishment at random, throughout their childhood. I did spank my oldest harder than I should have a couple of times, and Peter later exaggerated these incidents in court. I also yelled at my kids, during this time period, a lot.

. . . . .

To avoid isolation and to learn how to be a better stay-at-home mother, I started attending a Bible study for women in the community. I looked up to many of the women and I benefited a great deal from this group. Our study was quite rigorous, not unlike what our husbands were going through while they were attending seminary. The study leader believed in my good nature and talked with me frequently. To this day, words can't even begin to describe how much she helped me during those difficult years.

As part of Peter's degree, he had to acquire clinical hours. I learned of a free marriage counseling group that we could join that would help Peter to earn credits, so I signed us up. While attending this group, I started to feel that there were serious issues in our marriage and I started to speak up. Both the male group leader and the female leader validated me and my concerns. They confronted Peter about how he treated me and about his ongoing generational family issues. They encouraged us to continue to talk about *his* family. Before completing the group requirements, Peter forbade us from continuing to attend. Peter despised the female professor/group leader, and went on to disparage her, going above her head to her superiors. Peter did not like women who challenged him.

There was no intimacy between us; we weren't connected in any way other than our existence, financial desperation, and our children. I thought often about leaving him, even then. As with The Little Engine That Could, thinking just ain't enough. I was a prisoner in my own home [2].

6 JACK AND JILL

SHORTLY BEFORE OUR WEDDING, BACK in 1991, Peter's older brother, Jack, began dating the perfect woman. Jill is the youngest of six children. She came from wealth and was so refined and beautiful, she could, even now, marry into a royal family and grace the cover of *Vogue*. I loved being around her, but was overwhelmed by her confidence and poise. I felt insecure and unworthy of her friendship; I was very awkward around her. I loathed my pregnant body and wore mostly Peter's shirts and stretched out sweatpants. Jill was free, had disposable income, drove a fancy sports car and was the most confident woman I had ever met. She is also incredibly loving, kind, warm and generous. The Waltons adored her, while they despised me. They compared me to her, bought gifts for her, which they gave to her in front of me, and were attentive to her needs. Sundays began to center around Jill and Jack.

Jill was Canadian, so she came in for the weekends to see Jack. Jill would save the Walton's reputation; Jack and Jill would be the perfect couple and would finally overshadow the scandal that I had brought to the family name.

. . . . .

Jill and Jack courted for a couple of years, and when I say courted, this is exactly what I mean. They were perfect. They married when my first daughter was three months old. Their wedding was extravagant, with a reception at one of the nicest hotels in Toronto. After a year, they moved to Ottawa. Jill left her family and a blossoming career so that Jack could begin his political career. She later told me that this is when she suspected his infidelities began.

. . . . .

Years later, they moved back to Toronto, so that Jack could begin law school and they could start a family. Jill's father supported them financially during this time. Jack and Jill had a son with special needs; he would have unexplained random, often life-threatening seizures. Between the medications and seizures he had some developmental delays. When he was two, Jill became pregnant with their second son. As Jill's due date approached, her father passed away. Jill was unable to attend her father's funeral because she was at the bedside of her dying son; his last seizure had been so traumatic his recovery was not expected. Jack shared with the immediate and some extended Walton family the details of the child's tragic death—how he had been taken off of life support and how Jill had rocked him to sleep—in such an oddly unemotional manner that even Peter noticed his strange demeanor and commented to me.

Jill quickly became pregnant again. Shortly after the birth of her third son, Peter and I visited the family. I will never forget the way that Jack looked at Jill—with undeniable disgust at everything she said. It was the same look I had received, the same one that John routinely gave Elaine, and the same that I would observe, a decade later, passed from Peter's younger brother to his second wife.

· · · · ·

Jill confided in me that she knew in her heart and gut that Jack was having an affair, and she knew with whom. She said that she felt as though she were losing her mind because he was so skilled at convincing her that everything was her fault and at admonishing her distrust of him. It is the same cycle, shown in the figure one diagram, which I observed in John and Elaine's relationship. Jill had become "mentally ill," so Jack became further entitled to not only have the one affair, but to escalate into a heavy-drinking philanderer. Finally, Jill called a private investigator who set up a phone tapping system in their house. She recorded Jack having sexual conversations with numerous women. She confronted him and he confessed.

Soon after their son's death, Jack had begun an affair with a younger version of Jill. He blamed Jill for this, stating that she had not given him enough attention surrounding their son's death. She was emotionally unavailable to him during this time, so he felt entitled, and from there it had escalated.

When the Waltons turned on Jill, she shared the tapes with them. They still insisted that it was her fault. Jill and her family became a hot topic of discussion around the Walton dinner table and in the living room for hours in the evenings; to the point of obsession. Nearly all of Jill and Jack's friends sided with Jack. Even Jack's feminist cousins, who were in their wedding and were longtime friends of Jill's and of her family, turned on her.

The Walton story was that Jack had tried to win back Jill, but she had filed for divorce and moved on to another man. The Waltons, asserted that the new man was a domestic abuser, and feared that he was beating the two boys. They even sunk so low that they mocked his physical appearance, commenting on how much better looking Jack was, implying that Jack had always been better than Jill.

Through the years, she and I had become like sisters and I was close to her family. We looked forward to spending the rest of our lives in this way, appreciating the fact that it is a gift when sisters-in-law get along so well. She had to protect herself from the Waltons and their campaign against her. Wary of any communication with anyone remotely connected to the Waltons, she had to cut off from me as well; I was still a Walton.

· · · · ·

Nearly a decade later, when I was in crisis over infidelity and physical abuse, and determining if I should leave my marriage, she answered one of my attempts to communicate. *Had Jack ever apologized?* I wondered about that. He came to her door, shortly after she began dating the man who would become her husband. Jack had roses. He asked her to take him back and appeared shocked when she said no, a much different order of events than the Walton's claimed. I believe that he waited until he knew that she wouldn't take him back and made a big show, so that he could tell everyone that he tried. And it worked; he was seen as the victim.

Jill became a touchstone during my divorce and advised me that I had to get away, with or without my daughters. She said that she knew, firsthand, that the Waltons were alienating my girls from me. She also had to be careful as she still had shared custody of her two boys.

There are both similarities and differences between my story and Jill's. The most apparent difference is that though my mistakes are vast and obvious, she is truly an innocent victim. She is a beautiful and honorable woman who married the wrong person. She will bear the scars from Jack for the rest of her life. This book has been written, in part, for her, to clear her name. I love you, "Jill."

7 GUILT AND SHAME

MY CHILDHOOD LEFT ME WITH a great deal of guilt and shame. Because of this, I approached puberty with anxiety, an unstable sense of self and a distorted perception of my role in relationships. In other words, I was vulnerable to a predator. I was trained to devalue my needs and to give without question. I was conditioned to feel ashamed of myself and I went for long periods of time isolating myself, feeling unworthy of genuine human interaction. I felt guilt strongly and absorbed the wrongs of others. In my mind, they were not responsible for their anger, I was.

My cousin, the one for whom my uncle actually purchased the Darcy Barbie Doll, and for whom I have only the greatest deal of respect, managed to find and marry a good man. They married young, as well, and their intimacy shows after years of marriage. We have stayed in distant touch and she seems to have made it out from childhood with grace and has remained a beautiful person. My aunt, her mother, ended up finding a stable and downright good man; I believe he helped her get out of the marriage to my uncle. They thrive as a couple and raised my cousin and two other daughters who seem to all be lovely women. I'm thrilled that my cousin has flourished, created a beautiful family and become a strong woman of God. Perhaps I could have become the redheaded Barbie version if I had found comfort and support in loving arms or if I had been able to resist seeking these things from another. I'll never know.

In a loving, equitable relationship, the effect of my painful past would have diminished and, with the right help, it would likely not have affected me long after the abuse ended. Instead, Peter saw that I was raw, and took the opportunity to exploit my childhood abuse, constantly triggering me. [A trigger is an event in the present that causes a person to react as if they were experiencing a past similar event. Generally, it is seen as an overreaction and confuses others because the triggering event does not warrant the emotional response. [3]]

By being continually triggered, I became deregulated and I was unable to develop a stable and grounded sense of myself. In a loving, intimate, safe and secure relationship I might have developed a healthy, centered self and learned how to care for myself. Instead, I spent twenty years facing intensifying abuse.

When Peter and I returned from our honeymoon, we began a brutal cycle that accelerated over the years to come. There are disagreements in any relationship. When two people argue, they are

44

coming from two different perspectives, established by two different histories. It's critical to learn how to communicate effectively, to maneuver through the difficult times, back to a place of peace.

According to the book *The Verbally Abusive Relationship* by Patricia Evans, *"One of the greatest needs is to understand and to be understood." In a verbally abusive relationship, one partner's need to understand and be understood is not met. Her belief that her mate is rational and that understanding can be reached keeps her in the relationship. Not coming to this realization, however, leaves the victim living in an alternative reality where he/she is blamed for the battering of his/her own spirit* [4]."

Lack of validation in childhood, left me particularly sensitive to verbal abuse, especially not being heard. Peter used blaming tactics and then sat back and watched me unravel; then I became the problem. He judged and analyzed me, and his underlying issues got lost. He pointed his finger at me again and again; the problem was with me—every time.

According to Evans, *"When the verbal abuser refuses to discuss a problem, he prevents all possibility of resolution. In this way he exercises control over the interpersonal reality. Partners are frequently left with a sick, hurt feeling that is never really resolved. There is no feeling of closure. Upsetting incidents may reoccur in confusing flashbacks because they haven't been fully understood or resolved* [4]."

Einstein defined insanity as: *"Doing the same thing over and over, expecting a different result."* I attempted rationality and reason with a person who is incapable of either. I was slowly losing control of my mind.

"All verbal abuse is dominating and controlling. Verbal abuse used to control the partner without the partner's knowledge is called 'crazymaking.' The sustaining of power seems to be one key factor in crazymaking behavior. It appears to be a way of asserting dominance, while denying its existence or the wish for it [5].*"*

8 THE SOCIOPATH

WHEN YOU HEAR THE TERM sociopath or psychopath, you might think about a serial killer. That is one type, and there is another, more subtle type of sociopath, one that is every bit as destructive, one whose victim dies a slower, less obvious death.

I thought that my husband was a narcissist, or someone who suffered from an attachment disorder. Throughout the marriage, I periodically looked for material about narcissism. The consistent message I found was this: narcissists never change, they cannot change and I needed to get away as soon as possible. When our divorce proceedings began and he showed no regard for the safety and well-being of his own children, I realized I was dealing with someone who had no conscience, a sociopath.

· · · · ·

Peter enjoyed making me feel badly about myself. The worse I felt, the more power he had over me. I remember seeing the look of pleasure on his face, a smirk at times, when he was critiquing an interpersonal interaction that he observed. Under his constant watch, I would blunder my words and say stupid things. My inner worst thoughts would just spill out. I was ill at ease when we were with other people, definitely not myself. What I said, how I dressed, who I interacted with, what I liked and didn't was always about what Peter thought about me and how he felt I should best present my-self—never about me simply being myself. Now, I realize that I had been obsessing over the most normal interactions. Then, I just felt more shame and regret after interactions.

I remember playing the board game *Risk* one night, and Peter was "helping" everyone else, even though he was losing. I asked why he was correcting everyone else when he was the one in last place. Evidence doesn't matter to a sociopath. He responded that knew how to play the game "better than everyone." He had "special strategies." This is life with a sociopath. It doesn't make any sense. It is so contradictory and confusing that you wonder about yourself. If it's snowing outside, they'll tell you it's raining. They are so con-vincing that you start to doubt things that you can actually see.

· · · · ·

According to the book *The Sociopath Next Door* by Martha Stout, one type of sociopath is the non-ambitious type [6].

"You are the sort of person who really does not want much of anything. Your only real ambition is not to have to exert yourself to get by. You do not want to work like everyone else does... Without a conscience, you can nap or pursue your hobbies, or watch television, or just hang out somewhere all day long.

"Living a bit on the fringes, and with handouts from relatives and friends, you can do this indefinitely. People may whisper to one another that you are an underachiever, or that you are depressed, a sad case, or in contrast, if they get angry, they may grumble that you are lazy. When they get to know you better, and get really angry, they may scream at you and call you a loser or a bum.

"A partner does not have to be rich, just a financier that is reliably conscience-bound [6].*"*

In the twenty years that we were married, Peter worked for a total of about six years. In 2006, our fifteen-year-old daughter made more at her part-time job than he did—he did not make one dollar in that year. His idea of job hunting was to look at openings on the internet for about an hour, then return to television.

The economy (especially during the early 2000s) made it difficult to obtain a job, but this was different. This was like an outright revolt against working and helping to support a family. My stay at home mother days were short lived as Peter was unable to maintain employment—even part time. Ultimately, I ended up going back to school and working full time so that my benefits covered the school expenses. Peter did not look for ways to make my life easier, Peter only looked for ways to make his life easier.

. . . . .

There isn't a lot of information about sociopaths, but what I've found is a description of the man I lived with for twenty years.

Sociopathy, also called "antisocial personality disorder," is a condition affecting one percent of the adult population [7]. According to the *American Psychiatric Association's Diagnostic and Statistical Manual of Mental Disorders V*, antisocial personality disorder includes 1) ego-centrism derived from personal gain, power or pleasure; 2) impairments in interpersonal functioning including, a) lack of empathy, concern for feelings, needs or suffering of others, lack of remorse after hurting or mistreating another, and b) incapacity for intimacy or mutually intimate relationships, as exploitation is a primary means of relating to others, including by deceit or coercion and use of dominance or intimidation to control others; 3) antagonism using, a) manipulativeness to influence or control others, use of seduction, charm, glibness to achieve one's ends, b) deceitfulness by dishonesty and fraudulence, a misrepresentation of self, embellishment or fabrication when relating events, c) callousness or a lack of concern for feelings or problems of others, lack of guilt or remorse about the negative or harmful effects of one's actions on others, d) hostility with persistent or frequent angry feelings, irritability in response to minor slights and insults, mean, nasty, or vengeful behavior; and 4) disinhibition by, a) irresponsibility or disregard for and failure to honor financial and other obligations or commitments, lack of respect for and lack of follow through on agreements

50

and promises, b) impulsivity or acting on the spur of the moment in response to immediate stimuli, acting on a momentary basis without a plan or considering outcomes, and difficulty establishing and following plans [8].

. . . . .

With psychological conditions there's an ongoing discussion about nature versus nurture—genetics versus environmental factors. In Peter's case, I tend to believe that his transformation into a sociopath was mostly environmental. The bottom line: he didn't have limits, no rules that couldn't be broken and a stated and unstated sense of entitlement from a combination of his father's (and therefore the family's) status within their communities and his unique movie star looks.

I grew up with the Walton family. John's approach to parenting was to be absent as much as possible. Peter was basically fatherless. John's job required moving every two years or so. Peter was painfully introverted and did not make friends easily. He was also isolated. In his teenage years, Peter slept with a radio right next to his head; he played it loudly and rocked his own head to sleep. He needed to feel something, even if it was only the sound vibration and his pillow touching his face... side to side. He continued this habit throughout our twenty-year marriage. Peter had been neglected; I've always felt sad for young Peter. He often commented that he was raised by his older brother more than he was by his parents.

Elaine, having grown up in a highly-religious home with many siblings, was not raised with affection, and in turn did not provide a nurturing environment in John's absence. Peter recalled to me Elaine's constant migraine headaches, which caused her to spend days at a time in bed. I believe that she was depressed, married to an unloving man and raising three boys on her own. He also recounted that sometimes it was better—more relaxed—when his father was gone on a trip and they would sometimes even eat in front of the television.

Overall, she appeared to be going through the motions. She was not as educated as John, and had no other prospects of her own. Her in-laws had reminded her often that she was not their first choice; there had been a more sophisticated woman, a better match for their John. Her husband and sons were downright cruel to her, often offering nothing but disrespect and condescension. This cycle continued with me. The Walton home, in the years that I was a Walton, was unloving, cold, empty, unsafe and temporary, with the facade of classic perfection. One defining characteristic of the Walton men sticks out above the rest: *those men are the most insecure men I have ever known, with an insatiable need for validation from women.*

Peter should not have graduated from high school. He failed too many classes. John, highly attractive, charming and influential in the community, convinced the guidance counselor to let Peter walk. Peter pushed the edge of the envelope and learned that he could do whatever he wanted without consequence. As a child, Peter had the reputation of being the bad boy, which he maintained throughout his teenage years. In fact, his older brother would use him as "the muscle" and Peter was known for his fighting prowess. He is a violent person who engaged in fighting even after marriage and the birth of his daughter. I was embarrassed by his short fuse.

Elaine played the part of submissive wife without wavering. Without allowing room for her own thoughts, she automatically defended her husband and sons. I've seen the pain of captivity revealed in her eyes. The men in her life expect her to, metaphorically, lay herself down in submission so that they can climb on her back to reach just that much higher. They expect her to adopt their own perspective.

Elaine and Jill were extremely close when Jack and Jill were married; Jill was like a daughter to Elaine. Jill told me about a tear-filled reunion between the two after Jill and Jack divorced—they held each other closely, devastated over the unnecessary loss of their relationship. After this, Elaine was not allowed to continue to love Jill outwardly, Jill had crossed a Walton man.

9 YOU MIGHT BE MARRIED TO A SOCIOPATH IF:

IF YOU ARE HAVING A conversation and it is becoming increasingly apparent that you are right, a sociopath will suddenly change the topic to something that you've done wrong in the past. This is key—to stay in the past. The more painful the past, the more the sociopath focuses on it, especially if there has been failure or regret. There is no admission of fault on their part and no backing down. As flawed humans, we become more and more frustrated with the sociopath, unable to comprehend their twisted thinking. They talk over us never listening, much less validating; they change subjects quickly, escalating the conversation with assertions of obvious falsehoods with such intensity and venom we finally give up.

Any interaction, no matter how negative, will validate the sociopath, in their own minds.

They pick fights and antagonize just to get a reaction/response.

. . . . .

Peter would drive me to work and, just as we pulled into the parking lot, he would say something destructive and critical. I would then be on the phone with him repeatedly throughout the day, trying to resolve the morning's conflict. This happened regularly. After the divorce was final, I received emails trying to push old buttons in an attempt to engage me and keep me in the past.

. . . . .

You are exhausted and depressed when you are with a sociopath. You don't feel happy when you are with them.

. . . . .

Even on "date nights" I often ended up crying by the end of the night. Also on date nights, Peter walked ahead of me, leaving me looking and feeling very unloved, trying to keep up in heels.

. . . . .

There is always something wrong in the eyes of a sociopath—appearance, bad breath, what was said, imagined flirting.

You avoid a sociopath and when you do manage to get away for even a short period of time, you dread going back, sometimes becoming physically ill when returning.

The only resolution to conflict with a sociopath is to give in. If they are wrong, the conflict could go on for years unless you give in; it's frustrating because this is not resolution. You give in to end the conflict, often falsely owning up to something that you haven't done, and then that "false confession" is used against you in later conflict.

There will always be something wrong.

Sociopaths provide no evidence or documentation to back up their assertions and they ignore your documentation.

There is nothing you can say or do to influence a sociopath. If it seems they are absorbing something, it is manipulation; don't believe it.

Sociopaths present themselves as one hundred percent the victim and they twist scenarios into false realities. They punch you in the face and you apologize, just to keep the peace. This literally happened to me.

You never hear the following words from a sociopath: "You are making a good point," "I'm sorry I hurt you," "what can I do to help you?" "you look great today," "I'm so happy to be with you," "you are such a good mother," "do something for yourself today."

However, you do hear the following statements repeatedly: "You'll never find anyone better than me," "you'll never find anyone that will put up with you the way I do," "I treat you better and am better than anyone else you will ever find," "I take care of the house, I keep up your relationship with the kids while you work all the time," and, maybe unique to me, "I am so much better looking for a man than you are for a women."

There is no intimacy in relationship with a sociopath. They don't know what intimacy is, so they don't require a true connection, only control. You do not feel loved or cherished, safe or secure. They feel like an enemy.

As your children grow older, they start to treat you the way that the sociopath treats you. They slowly lose respect for you because they see you being continually disrespected.

Sociopaths are so judgmental and demanding that you are continually walking on egg shells.

· · · · ·

For twenty years, I was picked at, picked on and analyzed.

· · · · ·

Sociopaths initiate long discussions critiquing anything from parenting, to your work, to the way you brush your teeth.

They tell you how you think and feel, instead of asking. In fact, they don't ask many questions at all because they think that they know best.

There is no give-and-take, only taking. Sociopaths threaten you if they see that you might leave or are detaching emotionally.

. . . . .

In my case, Peter threatened to take my children from me and expose my mental illness. He only brought up alcohol as a problem after divorce proceedings started; Peter actually used alcohol systematically while interrogating me. He would bring me drink after drink, even if I refused.

. . . . .

When you do have time to take stock of your own life, you realize that you've lost friends and that you are isolated. Your time is primarily spent pleasing them. They don't like for you to spend time with anyone else.

Birthdays, holidays and special events are ruined. Sociopaths propagate drama.

. . . . .

One Christmas, Peter, who didn't like his brother Ben's first wife (a strong female), confronted her about her having been molested as a child (Peter thought that she showed signs of this, but had no proof). For the rest of the holidays, she did not come out of her room and the family and children were thrown into a very serious drama.

. . . . .

Sociopaths sabotage events that highlight you, the victim, or they demand that these events end unless they are somehow highlighted along with you.

. . . . .

Peter was upset with me the day I graduated with my doctorate, so we had to leave early; there was no celebration.

. . . . .

You can be in the depths of emotion and a sociopath looks at you with a coldness that runs chills down your spine. They don't have the ability to empathize.

There is emptiness behind their eyes. What they are saying often does not match the expression on their face and their eyes don't show emotion, except anger, their primary emotion. Sometimes, other emotions are misplaced because they are not really felt (i.e. they are overly dramatic about something that others find to be of little importance). Still other emotion is displaced or used as a tool to gain attention. It doesn't matter that by doing this, it lessens their respectability or natural shame, they do anything to get attention or sympathy as a victim (i.e. they get overly emotional at a funeral when they don't know the person; they see others getting attention and join in to the point of ridiculousness).

Sociopaths think that someone is always out to get them. There is always drama and over exaggeration. They talk about everyone behind their backs.

. . . . .

Peter forced me to relay everything that was said at even events like baby showers. He would decide that a friend of mine had wronged me and, by ignoring me until I acted, would force me to end the friendship.

. . . . .

They don't realize that they look weird to most people. Sociopaths live without self-reflection or acceptance of others' perspectives, thinking themselves better than others. They become disconnected from the norm and downright odd.

. . . . .

Peter's communications eventually emerged as "weird" to those involved in our divorce case.

. . . . .

Sociopaths don't see anything wrong with themselves, so they perpetuate an enhanced, grandiose sense of self.

If they work, they proclaim that they can run the business better. There is often a confrontation or conflict so that they have to leave the position or are fired.

. . . . .

At one job—the children's home that he would return to again later—after he was fired, Peter was escorted to his car, not even allowed a final interaction with his clients.

. . . . .

Sociopaths don't think about the future, not even when their present actions will obviously hurt them in the future. They don't consider future finances, only what feels good in the moment.

They cultivate the dependency of others on them.

· · · · ·

Peter wanted to always be involved with my work, he "helped" me draft emails—therefore needing passwords to my accounts—and tell me how to interact with colleagues; he even started to "proof read" other materials that I wrote.

· · · · ·

The general approach, interpersonally, is to be on the offensive and engage in conflict.

· · · · ·

There were many situations from which I wanted to walk away; Peter, and all of the Walton's, seemed to always be in a conflict. During our divorce proceedings, he explained my success and his underemployment by stating that he spent all of his time propping me up and that I could not have done it without him, that I had needed him all along. This argument has not held up; the farther away from him I get, the more successful I become. The best opportunities have emerged with so much more time to think for myself.

· · · · ·

Sociopaths prefer you dead rather than alive and sometimes they even state it.

They don't build up, they tear down.

You feel ashamed of yourself when you are with them.

. . . . .

Early in our dating relationship I did experience a moment where Peter seemed to be able to love me and express that love. I was sitting in the front seat while Peter's older brother was driving; Peter was in the back seat. I felt him looking at me and turned around. He was staring at me with a soft and loving look, like I was the only person in the world. This is the only time that I did not feel judged when Peter looked at me. His most frequent analysis when he looked at me from then on was that there was too much fat on my jaw bone. Even after years of disgusted looks, that one early look, that feeling of softness toward me, left me with hope that Peter could sincerely love me.

10 FINANCIAL ABUSE

WHEN DEALING WITH A SOCIOPATH, there is always financial abuse. For instance, when my oldest daughter was about to start first grade, Peter decided that I should homeschool her, due to a negative experience with a kindergarten teacher. A normal issue turned high pitch with a dramatic response. I had been looking forward to finally having a little freedom. I had planned to find part-time work and to catch up with friends. Peter could not allow this; he needed for me to be isolated and controlled. I was teaching aerobics part-time, and was given the opportunity to teach a class at a local college. It would've been so much easier on me to have the girls in school and not have to wheel them to work, in the wagon, and try to watch them while teaching aerobics.

Finally, Peter found a legitimate, full-time job making decent money that year. For once, we weren't living paycheck to paycheck.

Aerobics gave me an outlet, and a way to build self-esteem. The drawback? It was difficult juggling everything without a car. Still, I had a glimmer of hope. We had a three-bedroom townhouse with good neighbors and a safe area for the girls to play. I decorated their rooms like never before—one pink room, one purple. I ended up turning the purple room into a homeschooling room, full of charts and posters. Though frustrating at times, teaching her was a good experience, overall.

Shortly after, Peter's younger brother, Ben, found out about his wife's one time affair—the one who Peter had "diagnosed" as being a victim of child abuse at a recent Walton Christmas—Peter invited Ben to come live with us, encouraging him to leave his wife in the process. For an indefinite period of time, I would have Peter's un-employed, depressed, dependent little brother living in my home-school room.

When Peter was fired abruptly (from the children's home), it left five individuals under one roof, living off of only an aerobic instructor's "salary." I upped my classes to ten times a week, took a job at a local Hallmark store, started making wreaths on the side and would periodically give plasma. By the time winter rolled around, I had pneumonia. In the snow, I rode my bike to the local doctor's office and by the time I got there, I was unable to catch my breath from coughing. As I continued teaching aerobics, the pneumonia persisted. For months, I endured like this. I appealed to our pastor for help, and when he ignored me, we changed churches again.

Other seminary wives, also poor, gave us food and presents that year for Christmas for the girls.

Before he was financially secure, Ben moved out of our home and into an apartment down the street. He enrolled in seminary, instead of finding full time work, and hovered just above the poverty line. One benefit of his new living situation was that I was able to do laundry at his apartment; his apartment had hook ups for our washer and dryer, ours did not. He was kind and gracious the entire time—in our home and after moving into his own place.

I was offered a management position at the Hallmark store, and, at the same time, an entry level job at the nearby university hospital. The Hallmark position paid much more, but there was more growth potential at the hospital, so I took the full-time hospital job for minimum wage and benefits.

I started my master's degree at age twenty nine, when Peter already had two master's degrees. We paid full tuition for both of his degrees and had, at that time, about sixty thousand dollars of student loan debt. To prevent further debt, I needed a degree that came with job security. This time, instead of pursuing my dreams, I pursued a job where I continually saw job openings—epidemiology and statistics. My children's future was in my hands and my hands alone; and our overall financial future. My father, a former Marine, did not believe in carrying debt and he raised me to live below my means. I had expected to live like this in married life and assumed that my husband would consider my financial concerns and expectations.

I took a third shift position as a ward clerk, so that I could complete my homework at the hospital, and care for my daughters at home during the day. There were several of us working this shift for the very same reasons; we were all constantly tired and not living well. I slept, on average, four-to-five hours a day and Peter did not hesitate to wake me when he needed something.

. . . . .

Sleep deprivation is detrimental to the brain; it was difficult to stay focused in classes. When I began to perform poorly on tests, I had my IQ tested to determine if there was a problem. I scored in the top one percent of the population. I just needed to work harder and get a degree to earn better money. So, onto the proverbial treadmill I hopped. Peter said and did just enough to give me hope of change.

. . . . .

After about seven months, I was promoted to a research assistant position, with a regular schedule, both girls were in school and Peter found a teaching job at a private school. This was the most stable time in our relationship. We drove to work together and had a real schedule. We moved across town and were able to buy a home. It was small, but very nice with a very nice back yard and wonderful neighbors. I became friends with several ladies and overall, things were looking up.

This time I decided that I wanted another child; I wanted a son.

I soon became pregnant and I had never felt so good—physically, mentally and spiritually. I was part of a small group of women that met on Saturdays and I finally had close healthy friendships and support. I loved those Saturday mornings. Those ladies were my rocks during this period of time. At first I recoiled if they tried to hug me, telling them that they didn't want to do that, but I learned to accept their Godly love for me and their tireless support. The leader of the group, Patty, reached out to my oldest daughter, offering to be a mentor and informal counselor to her, to help her work through any difficulties. Patty became very involved in our family life, supporting and loving all of my children. She bought gifts, Bibles and expensive classic Christian books for my children and she spent a great deal of time just sitting with me and listening. She is very gifted in working with young women and in walking with them through the healing process—this is her purpose and ministry. I remember Patty saying that even she, herself, wished that her only daughter had a mentor like her. I wish I had listened.

Peter convinced me that Patty was hitting on him when the two of them interacted in my absence and that she was trying to come between my daughter and me—that she was a threat to me. He badgered me about Patty and about selfishness he felt that I exhibited by being in the group and spending time with any of the women. If I could have kept from listening to him and if my daughter had sought her guidance, to which she seemed open, I know that my dear friend, Patty, would've picked up on the alienation that the

Waltons brought to our family and she would have been able to help heal problems with my daughter and I, instead of the Walton's approach to completely cut off from me. She also could've filled the void I had made in the girls' lives, making them less vulnerable to the Waltons, and likely could have prevented their literal and emotional move away from me and to them. More than anyone else that I've come across professionally and personally, this is the woman who could've helped repair my relationship with my daughters.

I ended up doing what I had learned to do best: I harshly confronted her and abruptly cut off from all of them and from the group. I know that I hurt Patty and all of the other women deeply, causing a wound that, even when forgiven, would leave Patty needing to keep a safe distance from me. She has been very gracious to me in the aftermath of all of this and I appreciate any communications from her. To have lost Patty's generous friendship is devastating to me—a grave casualty.

During this time, Peter engaged in a hate campaign against the pastor of our church, where I had developed a community of support and belonging. The drama had become so intense that I became stressed to the point that I started to have pre-term labor signs. One day, I showed up at the school where Peter worked, thinking I should go to the hospital. I felt so uncomfortable watching him lavish his full attention on the young girls in his classroom—ages similar to his own daughters—right in front of me, while completely ignoring me. When I finally got his attention, we went to the hospital and our doctor determined that I was in labor.

I was given medication and put on bed rest. The pastor's wife and several women in the church, showing generosity I had never experienced, cleaned my house, did laundry, and took care of me while I was on bed rest. I carried my son to full term, but not without considerable, unnecessary stress.

. . . . .

We joined a new church, which met in the home of its pastor. Our old church community, who had been waiting to welcome my son into the world, saw me as the enemy because of Peter's pivotal role in the termination of their pastor. Once again, I was, for the most part, isolated and lonely.

. . . . .

Part way into my degree—and a few years of this new way of life—we learned that we could take out school loans for living expenses. Peter laid out a plan for him to stay at home with our son, instead of continuing to work at the private school. There was ongoing conflict and controversy between Peter and the headmaster—another authority figure—and Peter was miserable. This was the true motivation behind his plan. We had established a great schedule and situation; one neighbor, who had a daughter just months younger than our son, watched him for minimal cost, and Peter and I could continue to carpool. I argued and pleaded with him not to quit.

Peter quit his job anyway and we took out our first living expense loan—just to get us through while he looked for another job. Peter didn't just quit, though, he wrote a letter to the school's board of directors, scolding and belittling them. These were the wealthiest and best-connected people where we lived and he burned every bridge with his rooted pattern of claiming to be a victim and his insatiable need for conflict and chaos.

. . . . .

One day, following Peter's abrupt resignation, the gravity of our situation struck me as I drove home from work. The car's driver's side window was broken; the car, itself, was a gift from a seminary couple during our most recent desperate time. I was driving home in the pouring rain, drenched and crying. While stopped at a stop light, I felt people staring at me. Why had I put myself in this position once again? Why had I assumed a future of stability and normalcy?

. . . . .

I continued on after my master's degree and started my doctoral degree. I had received a full scholarship and an additional five hundred dollars, per semester, for books. I had to obtain permission from the graduate school every semester to be allowed to work full-time.

Peter never found that job and after one-hundred-fifty-thou-sand-dollars-worth of "school loan" debt (really living expenses debt), I completed my doctorate. We did not need those loans. We were paying back his school loans with my school loans, and he was spending three hundred dollars a week, just on groceries. He did not think ahead; he needed to feel good in the moment, and he knew that I would somehow bail us out. He really didn't care about debt, or even about filing for bankruptcy. A common conversation of ours was when we had only one hundred dollars until payday, I asked him to please only spend fifty, but he often spent two hundred and fifty without hesitation. We bounced checks every month. Finally, I opened my own bank account and managed all of our money, paid the bills, put out fires and attempted to invest for our future.

11 WITHHOLDING, THE SILENT AND MOST POWERFUL FORM OF ABUSE

HOW DO YOU "PROVE" THAT you are being abused when your husband systematically ignores you? In childhood, it is called neglect. In adulthood, it's lack of intimacy. It is abuse. Peter did not touch my face, kiss me for years at a time, or say loving things. He didn't compliment me or look at me during sex. His face most often displayed disgust.

"Disgust is the emotion that expresses a reaction to things that are considered dirty, revolting, contagious, contaminated, and inedible. It is divided into two categories: physical disgust and moral disgust. Disgust is associated with a distinct facial expression and a drop in heart rate [9]."

In my childhood and then throughout the years of marriage to Peter, I was conditioned to believe that I was a disgusting person. I reacted to touch like a beaten horse. I recoiled if someone tried to hold my hand or hug me. I had trouble giving affection to my children. I was disgusting; why would anyone want to even look at me? If Peter saw me naked, he looked disgusted. I covered myself; I was ashamed. He had been my first boyfriend, so I had nothing to compare to our relationship and I believed what Peter was showing to me every day. I believed that I was unlovable, and he told me that no one else would ever tolerate, in me, all that he tolerated. If I was not with him, I would be alone the rest of my life; I believed him.

When people in relationship experience tension, between coworkers, roommates, friends or neighbors, it brings stress into the body and the involved partied may dread interacting with one another. I lived through a marriage in which, if Peter thought that I made a mistake, he punished me by ignoring me. This disregard lasted for hours, days, or weeks at a time. I could not relax, fearing that he would ignore me. I changed myself in order to please him so that he would notice me. I stood at constant attention in my marriage; I did not ease into the safety and security of a loving partner. At times, friends and family questioned my quality of life. A couple of statements stand out: "When my husband and I get up in the morning, he asks me what he can do to help me and make my day go smoother," and "what does he offer *you*?" I could not imagine someone wanting the best for me: a giver, not a taker.

12 ISOLATION: PART II

IN THE ABSENCE OF ANY other relationship, you need them…
desperately. When you only have one attachment, their words and
behavior hold an incredible amount of power. Isolation of the other
is crucial to a sociopath. When the sociopath becomes your sole
attachment and then refuses to validate your feelings and thoughts,
you morph into a creature that is nothing like your former self. This
is also key for a sociopath: their partner is "crazy." As the victim
becomes more and more "crazy," without outside comparison/in-
sight, the sociopath is more-than-willing to offer "the explanation
and diagnosis." Bit by bit, they take your life. One day, you wake up
and there is nothing left of you; you are empty, lifeless, a dead shell
of a person.

· · · · ·

On several occasions, Peter suggested suicide—not his, mine. I was worth more than two hundred thousand dollars, dead. He would play the pitiful widower with a nice allowance for a while. Sociopaths thrive on playing the victim. Peter wrote a "novel" in which his first wife died by suicide. He talked about it with me in great detail and often, and I was in such misery that I thought about it, at times.

· · · · ·

I have two brothers. One is twenty-one months younger than I am. We are very close and always have been. We grew up in a rural community. Every day during our summer breaks, we played outside. Peter convinced me that this younger brother had been abused as well, and that because he had not acknowledged the abuse and therefore not gotten any counseling, he had become an abuser. Peter thought that our daughters were in danger, so I ended my relationship with my brother. Peter's abuse allegations were so far from the truth. Sociopaths don't operate in truth, they only operate within the false reality that they've constructed in their minds.

Sociopaths isolate their victims in subtle ways until the victim completely severs ties with all others to whom are close enough they might expose the sociopath. It's unnatural. My brother was close enough that he could have seen something wrong. If he had, he would have asked questions and defended me; before this had an opportunity to occur, Peter removed him from my life. After this, I didn't speak to my brother, or any family member, for four years.

13 HONOR THY FATHER AND MOTHER

Peter cut off his own friends and family, as well, eliminating all threats.

On May 9, 2006, Peter wrote the following letter to his father:

John Walton,

I am writing to respond to your unannounced visit last Monday. I want you to know that I in no way believe you to be repentant—you are a liar. Nothing in what you said suggested to me that you actually care about my well-being now, any more than you did when I grew up without your emotional presence. The cost of your self-worship is a son who doesn't desire relating to his father in any way. I believe you are a destructive influence on me and my family. I don't care if you believe otherwise; I'm not interested in any contrary evidence you might submit for consideration.

You are a tiny person, manipulating weak-minded people in order to per-petuate your own kingdom, which shields you from undesirable realities. I honor my father by telling you I utterly oppose you. I will not enter your kingdom ever again. You will not be permitted in my home again, and I will work to weaken your manipulative power whenever I can. I suspect you will not be able to keep your walls up much longer. All I encounter will know the truth about you.

I will explain to my children that their grandfather is not fit to interact with any of his grandchildren. Perhaps at your coming funeral I will explain the same to a larger audience: John Walton was unfit to deliver the gospel when he failed to receive the good news.

Peter Walton

Peter had severed relations with his family for years prior to writing the letter because, "John and Jack are narcissists." John Walton showed up at our house, unannounced, after we moved to Kentucky. Peter escorted him to the back porch and would not let him in. John had driven hundreds of miles to confess to numerous affairs, and apologize. This is the man to whom Peter turned when our separation became inevitable. John showed up in court proudly, standing by a son who discards people when they become unnecessary. John, Jack and Ben were eager to destroy me, with no consideration for the children.

By both Peter and I completely cutting off from friends and family members we thereby denied our own children relationships that might have been important to them; we trained them to behave in the same manner—this behavior normalized. Peter could easily manipulate them, given this conditioning, and use this as a way to "honor" me; by cruelly coercing his own children to sever all attachment to me.

14 THE TEN-YEAR MARRIAGE MILESTONE

ACTUALLY BEING ALONE WOULD HAVE felt less lonely than being with Peter. I constantly told Peter that I was vulnerable to other men. I craved their attention and I found myself flirting, hung up on every compliment that they gave to me. I was addicted to their attention and I mistook their signals as pursuit of intimacy. My only freedom was at work, so that's where I tested my boundaries.

. . . . .

When I was working overnight shifts at the hospital, a co-worker told me that a guy there had asked about her "hot" friend. After she mentioned this, I noticed that he was paying a lot of attention to me. We soon found ourselves alone and I remember the first time he asked if he could kiss me. By choosing to cross the line and not being coerced was a line that I had never before crossed and, from then on, it proved difficult to come back from it. Unlike my earlier infidelity with the woman, a predator using my vulnerabilities for her own gratification, I felt, this time, that someone really cared about me. He was kind, patient with me and not demanding—willing to just be with me, without expectation. I felt good for the first time in a long time. We fooled around for months until I was promoted. My promotion took me away from third shift and to normal business hours, we would not be in close proximity and would have to be intentional about continuing instead of "it just happening," so it ended. We didn't have sex, but my boundaries would not be the same again.

My father's love protected me from promiscuity until I met Peter, whose cold, unloving loathing made me vulnerable to himself and to others. The man with whom I fooled around was married; his wife figured it out what we'd been up to, and he lost everything. He and I have since run into each other a few times, and he is gracious, but very clear that he is keeping his distance. He is the first man to have treated me with respect and with what seemed to be love. I was so guilt-ridden that I confessed to Peter.

. . . . .

At one of the first conferences that I attended after being promoted to a research position, after the meetings, I had dinner by myself. I also had some wine. I noticed a moustached man hitting on a woman at the end of the bar. She was in her twenties, I, then thirty. She came over to me, sat down right beside me and ordered me a drink. She gave me her undivided attention and that got my attention. The man angrily said to me, "you cock blocker, bitch." I had no idea what that meant. She was attractive in her flannel, obviously not from the city, and she told me about her troubles with her philandering husband. She had started her own business, and when she found a conference for like-minded people, she registered. After meeting a man online, she arranged to meet him at the conference, which was just a cover. She told me that she worried that the birth of her daughter had stretched her out and that this new man would notice. She asked to go back to my room. Peter planted a seed in me that being with a woman was okay, and he encouraged it, at least initially, so I thought that this was safe and I longed for gentle human contact so much. We went to my room, watched some TV, I went to the bathroom and when I came out she was completely naked on the bed and became sexually aggressive toward me. I didn't want her to touch me sexually and stayed clothed, but I did get her off. I told her she was fine and shooed her out of my room. The next day, she pursued me intensely and she continued to pursue me, periodically, for months after. I ignored her out of shame; I wasn't even nice. I told Peter when I returned home and he was highly aroused, suggesting that I try it again and contact her. However, when he was in a position to use this against me, he did.

15 INFIDELITIES

ABOUT THREE YEARS LATER, AT another conference, a man looked at me and said, "Wow, I'd love to see you coming out of the shower every morning." I slept with him that night. Before this, I had not had sex with a man outside of my marriage—another boundary crossed. I was, once again, plagued with guilt. That particular compliment hit home. Exiting the shower was when I felt, particularly, that I disgusted Peter. After I returned home from the conference, I told him everything.

At another conference about a year later, on the last evening everyone was drinking a lot. I was, at this point, drinking to black out drunk regularly; especially when I was away from home and could escape from the stifling expectations and judgements.

As I began to come into consciousness I realized that two men were undressing me; they were trying to get me to sit up so they could take my top off over my head—commenting about me as they removed clothing. And next...one of the men was on top of me and he was having sex with me. The other man was sitting in a chair next to the bed and was watching. I screamed to stop and the older man pretty much ran out of the room. I begged them not to leave me, confused and looking to them to provide me some comfort. The younger, the one who was having sex with me, did stay, consoled me and helped me find my hotel room. He genuinely felt terrible and apologized many times; he thought I had wanted to do that and said I had told them "yes" initially. As I began to sober up I started to put the pieces together about what had happened. The older man was hitting on the younger man—he was a predator— the older man had orchestrated the incident so he could pleasure himself by seeing the young man in a sexual act. When I got home I sought Peter's comfort and we discussed if we should call the police because I was passed out. We didn't for several reasons: I believed I deserved whatever happened to me because I had put myself in an unsafe position and, secondarily, the older man was a public figure and the event would necessarily cause a great deal of media attention. Not only has this encounter damaged me psychologically, but the older man tried to damage me professionally for years after, disparaging me whenever possible. I was downright scared of him and thought some days he might kill me or have me killed—to protect that secret.

. . . . .

At a work meeting a few years later—I was thirty-six by this time—I noticed a young, handsome, single police officer checking me out. A few days later, he called me when he was drunk, and begged me to come to his apartment. I declined, but I was flattered by his generous compliments. I mistook his fleeting lust for loving desire. We began to talk on the phone every day. I dreamed of running away with him and almost did, but he was too young. I thought that I loved him. He told me that he loved me and promised to take me away and to take in my children. The fact that he was a police officer increased my attraction to him; I longed for safety and security. Though my relationship with this man was not sexual, I could not convince Peter of this. It was an emotional affair. Having confessed to sexual encounters in the past, I couldn't understand why he didn't believe me. I think Peter thought this man was a legitimate option for me and I might really leave this time. I ended all communication, but Peter continued to closely monitor me, even more than he had before.

Peter interrogated me in the evenings and he was so preoccupied by my life away from home that he bugged my car. I had no idea, and I assumed that he was merely intuitive as he repeatedly told me about myself. He finally revealed the tapping and told me that he would stay only if I went to intense therapy sessions. He discussed all of this with his then-therapist, Stan, and they decided together that it was best if Stan counseled me—they felt that I needed it more than Peter. Stan was not in our insurance network, so I paid one hundred fifty dollars, out of pocket, every week. After my initial intake, Stan insisted that I see him for an hour and a half, twice a week. I took out yet another loan, just to cover the cost of therapy. I should have left Peter. Instead, everything escalated. He would wake me in the middle of the night to interrogate me. He was more physically abusive than usual—Stan dismissed this. Peter told me, repeatedly, that I should have let him continue to be the bread-winner, even if it meant that we were homeless.

. . . . .

These infidelities were the basis for Peter calling me promiscuous during divorce proceedings. My immoral actions would cost me more than I ever could've imagined.

. . . . .

This went on for a couple years until Peter announced that he needed some time to himself—he moved out. He told me that he shared an apartment with a male co-worker (he had returned to a lower position at the children's home from which he had been fired, years before) who worked the night shift. This would allow him enough space to work through everything that I had done.

Peter rarely came home, and, when he did, he was usually hungover and sat around watching TV. This reprieve from him was wonderful. I had the house and children to myself, and I could parent the way that I wanted to. It was the most peaceful time I ever had with my daughters, and the healthiest. My youngest daughter admitted this during the divorce, though no one took note of this vital piece of information.

. . . . .

Though it may seem that this was the height of my oblivion, it got worse. I invited Peter home for an Easter dinner. He had been out of the house for a couple months at this point. He exploited my loneliness and my desire for touch. We didn't use protection and he made no effort to prevent pregnancy. I found out that I was pregnant a few weeks later and I called him. He coldly said that the pregnancy didn't change anything. Six weeks into my pregnancy, I learned I had a vaginal infection and couldn't get over it because of the pregnancy. In the store picking up a second round of medication, I called Peter and asked him if he had been with anyone else; he vehemently denied any infidelity.

My daughters rallied around me and even posted "Happy Father's Day" on my Facebook page. Peter didn't move back in, but came home periodically. His physical abuse continued to escalate. Without my knowing what I had said or done to upset him, he threw me down, pushed me, shoved me, grabbed me and choked me. Then, he abruptly left. I felt abandoned, over and over. I leaned heavily on my church and priest during this time. My priest released

88

me from the marriage stating Peter had abandoned his family. It was while I was in church week after week that I heard a voice in my head telling me over and over that Peter was a liar and that I needed to end the relationship and get my children away from him.

My oldest graduated from high school during this time. Peter was supposed to meet us at the ceremony, but he called while the rest of us were en route, saying that he wasn't able to make it. My daughter was devastated.

In my third month of pregnancy, I started bleeding. I called Peter and he said that he was busy, so I drove myself to the hospital. The emergency room staff was surprised that I had driven myself. Peter never asked me about this.

During my second trimester, I was at the doctor's office for an ultrasound; my son and Peter were with me. Mercifully, the baby was dead. I turned to Peter and said, "You are released. I'm done."

I had to have surgery because the baby wasn't being expelled naturally, and I needed an epidural. I had never had an epidural and I was scared. Peter refused to stay with me. I could tell that the anesthesiologist felt badly for me. In the recovery room, Peter busied himself by delivering chocolates to the nurses, then he left, only returning when it was time to drive me home. He dropped me off and then left.

That night, I started bleeding heavily and needed to go back to the ER. I called Peter, but he didn't answer. For the first time, I called the co-worker with whom Peter claimed he was staying. The man told me, realizing the weight of what he was revealing, that Peter had never stayed with him.

I knew.

. . . . .

I changed the locks and ignored his calls. I packed his things and, a cliché, threw them in the garage. Then, I left for New York to stay with family. While I was gone, he painted the garage as penance. He became the man I had always dreamed of—the one with whom I thought I had fallen in love in the first place.

When I returned home, I agreed to meet him at a public location. He confessed, but did not apologize. He asked me what he could do that would help me allow him to come home, and I suggested a men's therapy group. Therapy was always his suggestion for me. I think he went to the group only twice.

16 A DEVASTATING MISTAKE

AFTER MONTHS OF HIS PURSUIT, I did the unthinkable, a mistake that would dearly cost me and my children. I let Peter come back; he was chain smoking—a non-smoker until he left—and drinking hard.

During his absence, I made friends and began to build a life of my own. This is when the sociopath fakes love—when they sense that it's really over. Peter's loving façade lasted exactly two weeks. After that, he began to divulge details of his time with Charlene, the woman with whom he lived after he moved out. I became hysterical as he painted such a painful picture of his time away. On one of these occasions, I asked him—between sobs—why he didn't just apologize. He responded, "I didn't know until now that I had hurt you this much." In his mind, it was my fault that he hadn't apologized.

· · · · ·

Jill finally took one of my calls after me speaking with one of her sisters. At this point, I was sleeping in the closet each night. She said, "Look at you; you are sleeping in a closet with an unemployed man who has nothing to offer you…think about it…with or without your daughters…save yourself."

· · · · ·

Fearing my newfound independence, Peter escalated and I pushed back harder than I ever had. Peter obsessed over the idea of us engaging in a threesome, first with his mistress Charlene and then with one of my good friends.

17 CHARLENE

PETER IS SUCH A GOOD liar that I never suspected his living situation during the months that he lived with Charlene. When I questioned him, he made intense eye contact as he responded, instilling fear in me and distracting me from his lies.

. . . . .

After the two weeks of atonement, he showed no guilt. In fact, he looked smug when he talked about what it was like being with Charlene, and compared her to me: she was aroused all the time around him (I wasn't), he washed her long curly hair when they bathed together, they loved to drink and smoke on her apartment porch after work, he scheduled all of their shifts so that they could be together,

her young breasts, her aggressive sexuality, her confidence, she complimented him constantly...

Charlene had been quite upset when she learned that I was pregnant, and, after Peter returned home, she stalked me for a while. He was very bold during his affair, taking her out to dinner and meeting her friends. His brazen demeanor is another reason that I never checked up on him. I didn't pick up on any guilt from him because he wasn't feeling any.

HE took HER out to dinner. Peter bought my birthday gifts with my own money. Peter spent more of his "disposable" money on this woman than he did as a legitimate bill-paying contributor to our family.

. . . . .

One day, as I drove home from work, a car came up beside me; Charlene and a friend of hers honked, cut me off and flipped me off. When I got home, I told Peter that he needed to leave; I was fed up. He argued that Charlene would never do anything like that. He was still defending her after everything. That was it—there was my line. I was *finally* finished with Peter. That moment is very distinct in my mind; when I looked at him while he was talking, I saw him differently, I saw the lies and I saw the ugliness.

Peter, of course, had to quit his job because Charlene was his subordinate and he would be fired—twice from the same place—if they were found out. He quit so he didn't have to face further humiliation there. He asked me if he could stay until he found another job. I agreed to give him some time. I stopped drinking when Peter left, and I remained sober during the pregnancy and through the rest of the time that he was gone. When he came back, I started drinking again—a lot.

18 IF NOT BY MIND CONTROL, THEN BY FORCE

WHENEVER I DARED TO CONFRONT Peter, especially about his unemployment, this happened:

He grabbed me and took me upstairs to the bedroom. He got inches from my face and, in a growl, whispered that he would begin. I knew to be silent, to remain still and to look down in shame. "This is the type of treatment you deserve," "you are disgusting," "you do not know how to be a wife." After three or more comments, he pulled me to the ground and straddled me, he put his forearm on my throat and leaned in so that he was, once again, inches from my face and looking into my eyes. Then, he began with this phrase that will echo in my brain for the rest of my life: "YOU WILL SUBMIT TO ME." He said this while he pinned me to the ground; I could barely breathe. "You make me sick," "you leave a terrible taste in my mouth when you open yours," "this is how you deserve to be treated all the time." Sometimes, he then dragged me around the room by my feet, knocking my upper body into furniture, or he picked me up and pinned me against the wall. I was half his size and I let him do this, all the while thinking that I deserved it and that I needed to just take it.

Peter laid out my clothes; Peter told me to color my hair a darker, uglier color; Peter cut my hair; Peter packed my suitcases. He smelled my clothes, he checked my emails, he called me constantly at work and he analyzed me every minute of every day. He was never far from me. This is not love; this is one person controlling another, the opposite of what is natural. This is not a life worth living.

. . . . .

I've thought about my adulteries and, over the years, I've beaten myself up with my own inflicted guilt and shame. While writing this book, and seeing my life, during this time, in its entirety, and not in parts, I'm understanding myself and my choices better. At that ten-year marriage marker, I crossed a line with the man from the hospital. Also, at the ten-year mark, I became more confrontational and the desire to leave started to grow within me. I had no experience dating anyone else when I met Peter. I hadn't had the chance to discover anyone else when I was the age that most people are exploring their romantic options. A full decade into my marriage, I acted like a teenager, rebelling from a controlling husband who forced me into the role of a child with him as parent. But even with this new understanding, I have still damaged my psyche.

19 NEGOTIATING WITH A SOCIOPATH:

THE SUBMISSION PRINCIPLE

"DEATH DOESN'T COME UNTIL THE end of my guests' visits here, after I've grown weary of them. It's always so fascinating to see their disappointment." "Disappointment?" "Exactly. Disappointment. They imagine that if they please me, they'll live. They adapt to my rules. They start to trust me and develop a certain camaraderie with me, hoping to the very end that this camaraderie means something. The disappointment comes when it finally dawns on them that they've been well and truly screwed...."

"You see. You've already started to adapt to the submission principle. I hold your life in my hands....You pleaded with me to improve your quality of life, and you did so by using reason and a little good manners. And you were rewarded [10]."

I thought that it was normal to wonder when my husband would kill me and I thought that I deserved it and that my family would be better off without me. I know that he wanted to kill me because we would talk about it. I know exactly how he wanted to do it: he would strangle me to feel his power over me and my life. I thought that this was *normal*.

. . . . .

In April 2012, I blogged: "As soon as I said it was over that desire in him has only increased; I've seen it in his eyes. His internal rage toward me ebbs and flows, unpredictably, and actually silences produce my greatest fears. I'm thankful he and his family are not able to save money because, for now, their credit seems to have dried up or I would still be in court. I avoid communicating with him as much as possible, but then every month or so I have some sort of interaction where I could gauge his current level of internal rage and understand my level of danger. I learned to predict him somewhat by staying as emotionally distant and logical as possible; I'll never understand his thinking or actions, but I do have enough of a history that I know what to look for and sometimes can stay a step ahead. I have had to train my brain to react differently than with anybody else. I never think that what I say or do has any influence over what he will say and do. I try never to be influenced by an "act of kindness" or engage with cruel comments. This is difficult to do, but essential when dealing with a sociopath. I give him as little information as possible and try to never antagonize him.

There is not nearly enough information about sociopaths who live among us, but what information I have found is so disturbingly consistent and similar to my experiences that when I read I become physically ill, my circulation decreases so that I'm very cold and my body starts to tremble. I am fearful simply reading and remembering painfully similar information; this fear has been instilled over decades and will be difficult to change. Others have said the same thing to me about my story. If you've had dealings with, and been affected by, a sociopath it's difficult to not become afraid again. I still fear him and I can hardly believe I lived so intimately with such wickedness."

20 EVERYTHING IS MY FAULT, EVEN THE ABUSE

THERE WAS A GREAT DEAL of conflict throughout my twenty-year marriage, mostly typical problems: sex, money, in-laws and children. However, we were not a team, not ever working toward resolution or negotiation, not working on a marriage or partnership. *He had ulterior motives; his insatiable needs, expectations and desires were always shifting.*

. . . . .

He often involved our girls in our fights. Right before he moved in with Charlene, we began fighting over his desire to become a massage therapist. He had recently been demoted at work and he felt that the lower position was beneath him; he was humiliated to remain at the children's home. My concerns about his pursuit of yet another certification, "licensed massage therapist," were twofold:

more time without employment and the huge expense of pursuing the trade in the meantime. As outlined in figure one, he did not consider or even deign to hear my concerns.

The argument about his latest scheme ended with him dragging me around the house by my feet, straddling me, choking me, and growling degrading and belittling statements inches from my face. I was in bad shape, crying, yelling and fighting back. This time, however, I called the police. He woke my oldest daughter out of bed and brought her downstairs. He grabbed my face and told her to look at me and to notice how out of control and emotional I was. He told her to look at him and to notice how calm he was. He went on to tell her that her mother was disturbed and crazy, and that he had no choice but to restrain me in order to protect himself. All the while, he asked her to nod, to show him she understood.

My attorney says that even police, typically, still don't understand domestic violence. Of course the abuser is fine, he/she controls and abuses another person, while remaining calm and stressfree. Meanwhile, the victim is unheard, controlled, scared, upset and traumatized. The victim is the one who appears to present the problem, as I did, here, with Peter. This situation played out, exactly in the same way, with my oldest daughter at least a dozen times over the years, starting at a very young age. My younger daughter heard the escalated fighting, though she only witnessed it the few times that her father also brought her out of her bedroom to look at me. She heard me yelling the loudest. Peter generally remained calm; his abuse is very quiet, subtle and difficult to prove. My role in my own destruction was to be pushed to lose control, emotionally, in our home.

Peter, desperately, told our oldest daughter that it was up to her to prevent her dad from going to jail. He told her exactly what to say. When the police arrived they separated us. I was taken outside, in the dark; Peter stayed inside with our daughter. The police "did not see any bruises," (they developed later on my arms, legs and neck—and how could the police see anything without light?) and my daughter did as Peter instructed, so he was only sent to a hotel for the evening.

The next day I called him and apologized, begging him for forgiveness. I felt that I was the one who was wrong because I was *emotionally out of control*. This is embarrassing, but my response is typical of long-term abuse. He agreed to come home under the condition of my "complete submission" to him. He also said, "if you ever call the police again, I will take your children, all the money, the house…and it will be very easy to do considering your mental illness." I was on my best behavior.

· · · · ·

By the end of our marriage, my middle daughter, along with Peter, would regularly mock me and laugh at my parenting when I attempted to discipline her. Our interactions became volatile, in part, because Peter treated them more like the spouse and they treated me like the child. Our family dynamic became very confusing and dysfunctional; I was in a romantic/love triangle with one of my daughters. My older daughter remained open-minded and defended my work inside and outside of the house. Peter parented her in an entirely different way than he did our other two children; he was very hard on her and controlling, making her work at a very young age; his disciplines to her were often unreasonable and severe. However, by the time we got to court, she had turned against me with such vengeance that it took my breath away; I was blindsided.

This did not happen overnight, *and I unwittingly assisted Peter in my own destruction.* Peter used the girls as pawns, cultivating their worship of him. He was special; he had special powers to understand people and powers to correct situations. There were no jobs or churches or environments that were good enough for him. Not even his family was good enough for him, until he needed their help to destroy me. He persuaded the girls, directly and indirectly, to be antagonistic toward me, to confront me, both independently and along with him. Regardless of my actual mental state, if a family member has a mental illness, the family should rally around the sick member, certainly not use it against them. Now, I see that, over the years, my daughters slowly lost respect for me. Peter contradicted nearly every parental idea I had, relaxed my attempts to establish order and explained to the girls that I didn't know what I was doing; they just needed to do as he said. He convinced us all that he was the better parent. If our relationship had been a partnership, not his attempt at absolute power and control, we would have been united, he would've built me up and supported my parenting, expressing appreciation for my work and for my sacrifices for the family. While I worked so much, especially in the end, it was easy for him to turn the children away from loving and respecting me, as their mother.

21 IS LOVE REAL?

I TAKE OUT OF TOWN business trips, at least once a year, as part of my job requirements. While on a trip, in March 2010, I met Steven. Steven was visiting the same city as part of his job requirements. He was not staying at the same hotel as his colleagues, so he chose to interact with my coworkers during the hotel happy hour. I walked by the group; the difficulties between Peter and me were the centerpiece of my life and I was not interested in anything "happy." I was miserable and distrustful of everyone, and I wanted to politely greet my friends and quickly retreat to my room to have some quiet, no-drama time. During the pleasantries, Steven asked one of my colleagues for an introduction. I was introduced as Dr. Walton, director of a state program; this intrigued Steven. A dozen of us started talking and continued for hours. I learned that he taught mountaineering and remote-location survival. We all worked in violence prevention, so I posed this question to the group, "if you had a terminal illness and were in the last days of life what would you do?" Answers included: right wrongs, go places and some other standard responses. Steven responded, "I would want to free fall into the middle of Mecca during Ramadan with a man-pack-nuc (a back pack size nuclear device), because it would be nice to play by their rules." Perhaps, I could have guessed his real profession at this point; none-the-less, I was intrigued.

The next night, during happy hour, a colleague-friend of mine and I were having a private conversation. She, and two others, had been a tremendous support during the previous year when, at the same conference, I was pregnant and dealing with Peter's abandonment. I shared with her everything that had happened and she was horrified. She told me that she hoped to find love, but was being careful for some of the same reasons that I had just shared. She said that she would know with just a hug; it is the hug that tells everything, not a kiss, a hug. Steven was getting ready to leave the bar to have dinner with his friends, saying that he would be back. As a joke, I said, "Hey Steven, come over here and give us hugs." He was more than happy to oblige; he had rarely stopped staring at me in the time since we were introduced. It was a look like the one Peter had given me just that once, but Steven's carried with it more intensity and confidence than I had ever known. He waited to hug me last and when we touched it was electrifying. The hug itself—fireworks. I sat down, stunned. I turned to my friend and she said, "I know. I saw it." And after what Peter has done to you, you need to see if this is right and go for it. You might not have another chance if you wait, with him living in Alaska." Steven and I made love that night. It was different for both of us than it ever had been before. We fit perfectly together in every way. It was a beautiful connection, deeply unspoken. Our understanding of what happened would take years to rise to our conscious minds. It was serendipitous—love at first sight.

At lunch the next day, our conversation continued, but turned toward our difficulties with our soon-to-be (or so we thought) ex-spouses. He was living at his "school house" in a closet-sized room; I couldn't get my spouse out of the house and I had been advised not to leave, myself. Though we lived four thousand miles apart, our chemistry was so intense that there was a sense between us that, somehow, we would be together. That first "happy" hour was the happiest hour I'd had in decades. Several days later, Steven and I parted. Knowing that I was heading back into chronic and acute drama, chaos and fear, all without Steven's protection, I deleted his number and messages. I thought that I'd never talk to him again, but I couldn't stop thinking about him, so, after a few weeks, I checked my cell phone bill for his number and called him. It was so comforting to hear his voice. We had an immediate understanding of each other; we were going through the same difficulties with our spouses. If anything bad happened, my first thought was to tell Steven, and his first thoughts were of me. We helped each other, day after day, as we struggled through the worst times in both of our lives. We went back and forth, helping each other defend ourselves against a legal labyrinth of accusations that our spouses threw at us. Our soon-to-be exes were extremely similar, like they were reading from the same playbook.

. . . . .

Once, while I was on the phone with Steven, I walked through the house and when I came into the kitchen, where Peter was, I didn't stop talking. He asked me who I was talking to, and I told him that it was a man that I had met on my most recent work trip and that we were friends. Peter, of course, became suspicious. I did not hide my relationship with Steven from Peter. I ended up boldly telling Peter about my sexual encounter with Steven and how much better, overall, Steven was for me. I said, "I found better and I want you to leave. I'm not willing to wait for you to find a job." During the month after Peter returned to the house, I slept in closets and in a downstairs office; I was truly scared of him. His abuse escalated as my self-esteem, boldness and emotional detachment from him increased. He knew that I was done with him. For the first time, things were different.

. . . . .

In September 2013, I blogged: "They are both still obsessed to this day: they despise us; "sacrificed" to be with us, because all others

110

were better; and found nothing to love about us, even so they continue to try and ensnare us; anything to keep communication going. Their desire to control and hurt us, years later, is still as intense and as strong as the grip of eagle's talons. This is in and of itself quite a bond and at first I thought we clung to each other, thousands of miles away, because of our common anguish, but as time went on I realized our relationship was much more than that. I honestly don't think I would've had the strength to fight the court battles I did without Steven; the Walton's are too strong of a force when crossed. So when I learn of a women, or man, fearful to leave, I understand, it's nearly impossible to get away from a sociopath, especially at the beginning when you still believe you are worthless, fear the unknown and people in general, and have no sense of who you are."

22 THE CSI EFFECT

DOMESTIC VIOLENCE HAS BECOME MORE readily acknowledged thanks to a force of passionate researchers and courageous victims. In today's world, something exists called the "CSI Effect," where juries expect some sort of biological evidence in order to convict; eyewitness accounts and testimony no longer hold the weight they once did. I am thankful that he hit me in May 2010, hard enough to leave evidence.

. . . . .

Peter was obsessed with a particular friend of mine. She and I were very similar and we had chemistry; we fooled around a few times. Peter pushed me, hard, to pursue her; his only requirement was that

I tell him every detail. He found out that she was performing at a local restaurant and wanted to go, so we went. He drank heavily and kept trying to get her to come home with us and pushing me to hook up with her. He had bought new pillows and bedding for our guest room so that she would be comfortable and have the best. It was embarrassing.

That night, I was very upset, embarrassed, and I felt badly about myself, inadequate next to Charlene. I started screaming at him about how he wanted her more than he had ever wanted me. She had gotten what was withheld from me for most of my life. I was out of control with emotion. I was in the closet, on the floor, next to all of our shoes crying and rocking in the fetal position. Peter was standing in the doorway, which trapped me in the small room. I remember just wanting to hurt myself. I took one of Peter's dress shoes and began to beat my vagina with it, trying to insert it. He grabbed me, threw me on the bed, straddled me, his knees pressed on my arms so I couldn't move or protect myself and punched my face several times, close-fisted.

The next morning, I was very bruised and swollen and I tried to hide it from our neighbors (there was a neighborhood garage sale that day). Peter's brother and wife came over that day. The two of them initially believed me and supported me.

Two days later, Peter threatened me saying that it would be easy to take the children from me if I tried to kick him out before he found a job. I went up to the bathroom, locked the door and took pictures of myself. I had bruises in my ear, my eye, on my lip and all over my arms. I had the sense to take pictures, knowing that I would divorce and fearing all of his threats. I am thankful that he hit me—physical abuse is really the only abuse that our society recognizes. Outward anger is the main thing that identifies a perpetrator, not the subtle, controlled, most wounding manipulations.

Peter was unpredictable and I started to feel that I was being set up. I might need those pictures in the future, as proof of his abuse.

23 PETER FINALLY LEAVES

THINGS ESCALATED QUICKLY AFTER THE night that Peter punched me. When one of my cousins learned that I could not get him to leave, she planned a visit; our daughters are the same age and they seemed to get along very well. My cousin has a very strong personality and Peter knew that she was not pleased with him—she was the one I visited after learning of Charlene. Peter only bullies those whom he has under his control; he did not have her under his control and I believe that he was afraid of her. I was emboldened by her impending visit; I told Peter that I no longer wanted to be responsible for him. His family, those who had created him, could take care of him. I left the house, telling him to take whatever he wanted; I just wanted him to leave. He moved into an apartment down the road from our house, just days before my cousin's arrival.

He said that I would not be able to function without him. I responded that I'd be okay picking up his one load of laundry a day. My last words were, "I never wanted to marry a weak, needy, unemployed man."

That weekend my neighbors' teenage kids had a party. They had parties often and I was generally the one who stayed up, monitoring, while Peter went to bed. My daughters are close to the same age, so they had some of the same friends. Peter thought that I was too harsh with the girls about drinking. He thought that it was fine for them to drink, as long as they were at home. My cousin let her daughters, all of whom were underage, drink. She and her oldest made *Jello* shots for the weekend. I did not have my son with me for the weekend, but knew it was a bad idea. Still, I didn't stop any of this. Neither my cousin nor my neighbors had ever gone through anything like what I was going through, so they thought that I was overreacting. I was very nervous about Peter; it was becoming obvious to me that he had a plan. The evening that my cousin arrived, Peter picked up our son for the weekend. Peter blamed me for the neighbor's party, taking an opposite stance to the one he had taken in the past. My son later revealed to me that, during this time, his sisters were disparaging me and trying to convince him to leave with them, so that all of them could live with Peter.

My cousin was shocked at the way my daughters spoke to me. She confronted them, saying that they should not talk to me so disrespectfully, she defended me. It was too late. The seeds had been sown and now everything that I did—good or bad—would do further damage. My oldest left shortly after this weekend and never returned to live in my home again. These were the final days of our relationship.

24 THE LAST DAYS

MY LIFE WAS LIKE A train without breaks, racing down the tracks. Peter had planned ahead so that he could just sit back and merely push the buttons. The Waltons had brought my oldest daughter in close to them. In a few months, she transferred from a college, which I was paying for, in close proximity to me to a college close to the Waltons. The University where I worked happened to be a perfect fit for her talents and career ambitions; tuition would have been free and she could have lived with me. To encourage her to go elsewhere was not in her best interest. Peter had turned my younger daughter into a spouse; he manipulated her by confiding in her about adult matters. By exposing her to "our marital issues," making her feel important by disclosing sensitive and private information, she became his advocate and caregiver, and I became the enemy. This is the Waltons' craft, something I saw played out by more-than-willing victims, desperate to be a part of the Walton inner circle. I had no chance with either daughter and the last days solidified our end.

. . . . .

Sometime after Peter left in June and before the end of that July, my daughters were at the house. Peter and I had worked out how to split time with the children (and, really, everything else) by this time. My younger daughter was supposed to stay with me for the weekend. She was becoming unmanageable, arguing Peter's lines in his absence. She wanted to go out with friends and I said no. She started to scream "I want my daddy!" over and over, so loudly that the neighbors commented about it to me the next day. She called him and I took her phone. Finally, I was able to maintain control of my own emotions. I was in disbelief and completely helpless, I had not developed skills to counter outburst.

She escalated emotionally, screaming more loudly. My oldest started to yell at me that I was out of control. Peter and his brother were parked, conveniently, at the opening of the cul-de-sac, something my neighbors later told me that he did often after he had "left." Peter called the police. When they arrived, my oldest daughter kept yelling that I was out of control; the police responded that the girls were out of control. They ordered the younger one to go to her room and the older one to leave the room. They told me that I was in a tough spot and that I needed to think about my minor son, advising that it would probably be best to let my youngest daughter go to her father's house to avoid further accusations against me. While the police stood in the doorway, I called my youngest and told her to pack; she was going to live with her father. I helped her to dump her things in plastic totes and she left; my oldest left with her. He had them now, I was helpless and hopeless. These were the final days of our relationship.

This was one of the most traumatic moments of my life; I've had trouble remembering it because it was so traumatic. I felt a loneliness and emptiness that left me frozen, not knowing what to do. I had not been without my children since I was nineteen years old. I'm not sure about the timetable, whether it was the same night or days later, but I did call Peter. I yelled at him, telling him that I would formally file for divorce. I was fed up, I ranted at him and, of course, his brother, Ben, was with him and heard it all. I believe that this conversation was the final nail that he needed to seal my proverbial coffin. The worst was yet to come.

25 MY WORST FEARS

July 2010

PETER WAS GONE, AT LAST, or so I thought. One night a few weeks later he threatened that he would still "come and go into the house as I please, the police told me I have that right." The morning after his threat, I filed an Emergency Protective Order, knowing that recent separation with impending divorce is the time in which most intimate partner homicides and homicide-suicides occur. I truly feared for my life and even had friends stay in the house with me during this time. I didn't try to damage him by restricting him at our place of employment (I had gotten him a part-time job where I worked my second job), because other people were around, and I didn't involve the children. I simply did not want him in or around my home. I filled out the paper work, the family court judge saw me and a hearing date was set for a week and a half later.

. . . . .

What happened on the day of the hearing, still sends electrical currents through my body. He appeared in the courtroom in a new suit, with his father and two brothers, also in suits. My former therapist from 2007, Stan, and an attorney were also at his side. This was the beginning of the set-up: *in cases of custody, no records are confidential, all parties have full access to therapy records, medical records and any others.*

In the courtroom, sitting with a social services advocate, I was served a thirty-five-page motion and an Emergency Protective Order filed against me, "protecting" my abuser AND my children from me. The motion contained every bit of information that could humiliate me, gathered across the twenty years of our marriage; he did not hold back at all. He took nuggets of truth, sometimes just the frameworks of events with no regard for the truth, and embellished them to a degree that they no longer resembled reality: they were HIS reality, only. He accused me of the mental illnesses that, apart from schizophrenia, are most damaging in child custody battles. He accused me of alcohol abuse and of abusing all three children. My eldest (nineteen years old at the time, coincidentally, the same age that I was when I became pregnant with her) signed an affidavit saying my son (six at the time) should not ever be left alone with me; my abuser should have *sole custody*.

He sought *sole custody*, my retirement, child support of fifteen hundred dollars per month, most of the furniture in the house, the car and alimony. I learned, later, he had secured moving trucks and had planned to move back to his family in Canada that day. I also later learned that my daughters' cell phones, which I had purchased and was maintaining, were turned off and that the Waltons had purchased new phones for them, with new numbers, so that I would not be able to reach them. I noticed on social media that they had new clothes; the Waltons were buying them off in an attempt to captivate and capture them.

As I read, I realized everyone in the courtroom was watching me, waiting for my reaction. I realized, in that second, that everything in my life could be taken from me. My worst fears were becoming MY reality. Everything depended upon my reaction. I did not cry, I kept a stoic face, I looked straight forward and I did not talk to the social worker, I simply passed the papers to her and I waited.

Peter and I were called up to the tables, much like in the show, *Law and Order*. His entourage sat directly behind him. I sat with my social worker, who was younger than me. His extremely aggressive attorney began by asking for the first witness to be called. They were going strip me of everything. I raised my hand and waved it a little and asked his honor if I could be heard. As Peter's attorney continued to bellow, I stood.

The Judge stopped his attorney and I said, "What is about to happen is unfair. I am asking that your honor give me time to obtain an attorney to fight these false accusations and prepare a defense." The Judge agreed and began the discussion of foster care. He asked if there was any person on whom Peter and I could agree to watch our six-year-old son and our sixteen-year-old daughter. We agreed on the children's godparents and I called them. Thank goodness, Susan answered the phone and agreed to take the children. I had one week to fight.

I wish that I had known more about divorce and custody cases. No one talks about it. Everyone talks about planning a wedding; I had never come across anyone who was planning a divorce and talking openly about it. I now know why no one talks: it is a public failure and it can be such a traumatic process, that when you finally get out, the last thing you want to do is re-live the experience by talking about it. Writing about my experience is difficult, but I feel compelled to make my story available to victims who are thinking about leaving a narcissist, a sociopath, or any sort of abuser. It's not ever easy, but we can take steps to make it easier. Please learn from my mistakes—I have made so many.

. . . . .

As I left the courtroom, a woman that I didn't know pulled me into a side room. She was a domestic violence advocate and had been sitting beside the Judge. She told me to stay in the room, that I could not leave at the same time as Peter. She observed that he was acting like a typical abuser and that my safety was at risk. I broke down and began to sob uncontrollably. She left and brought back with her a female attorney and a female police officer. They explained to me what was happening.

They explained that abusers plan ahead; he had probably been planning this for years and it would take an enormous amount of energy, discipline, money and time to turn the court in my favor. This is what happens to victims: we look crazy because we don't expect our loved one to turn so quickly and with such venom. It catches us off guard. We have spent years defending our abusers and blaming ourselves—to change this distorted thinking is nearly impossible. Sociopaths thrive on the unpredictable and on destabilizing their victims. This was completely unexpected and I was destabilized. We cry, we yell, we panic; at the very least, we become so anxious that we cannot hide it. Our babies are ripped out of our arms, our deepest, most intimate moments/mistakes are exposed to the public and hard-earned money taken from us. Our worst fears are realized. The advocate, in an attempt to encourage me, said that she had never seen a domestic violence victim remain so composed; generally, we lose control, lending credibility to the abuser's claims of mental illness.

. . . . .

Show no emotion and say as little as possible

. . . . .

The attorney, police officer and advocate began to search for an attorney to help me. They gave me the names of two attorneys, one,

125

an expert in dealing with domestic violence cases ("the best"), the other, the former county domestic violence prosecutor. When I left, I could not go home. I had not lived alone for decades. My three-thousand-square-foot home was empty and I didn't know what my abuser was capable of; he had just shocked me in court. My son was at his godparents' house and I was not allowed to see him; I could only call him. How was he dealing with this? My abuser had isolated me, had left me with a negative checking account balance and no credit cards. I was broke and I had no idea how I would come up with a retainer for an attorney. I wandered around the local mall in a daze.

I felt completely alone. I had not talked to my family in more than four years. If I did nothing, Peter would take my son to Canada, much of my retirement would go to the man who inflicted years of financial suffering on our family and I would pay an incredible amount of child support. My abuser and his family would take everything. Their complete disregard for the health and wellbeing of their grandson still utterly astounds me. The saddest thing that I've learned by telling my story is that I'm far from alone. Our stories, as victims, are eerily similar.

. . . . .

I called my brother. He didn't answer, so I left a message: "I know we haven't spoken in some time so you understand that this is an emergency. Please call me back, please." Then I called Cassie, my best friend from childhood, the one who had let me borrow clothes before seeing Peter, and I asked if she had any contact with my brother. She said that she had connected with my brother's wife on Facebook and that she would try to get in touch with him. She left an urgent message for him. She could not believe what was happening to me. Peter's family was a *"perfect"* family.

Things were becoming very clear; this storm was *too perfect to not have been planned.* Peter had insisted that I cut off from my family, so I had no familial resources; I could not turn to them. He had spent down our account, leaving me with nothing. He had made it so difficult to maintain friendships that I didn't have anyone to whom I could turn for financial help. He, on the other hand, suddenly had the full support of a brother working in Canadian politics, one who was making an excellent salary, along with the support of his parents and a younger brother.

Cassie stayed on the phone with me as I aimlessly walked around the mall; she was worried. The mall was closing and it was time to go home—*alone.* When I walked through my front door, I was afraid for my safety. A wave of nausea swept over me, then another. I didn't know if I could bear the burden of this pain, injustice and helplessness. I did not know if my mind could handle it.

I called Susan, I was sobbing, I wanted to hold my baby, my little boy. She was immediately "on my side." She saw what was going on and had seen it for a while. For the next year, she and her husband were two of the few people who saw the truth.

. . . . .

I finally slept, but woke up full of panic and anxiety. I was not going to lose my son! I got in touch with the first recommended attorney, but it wasn't a good fit, so I called the other, the former county domestic violence prosecutor. It took another full day before she got back to me, but it was an immediate fit; she made herself available to me and my case. I told her that I was working on getting some money together.

My brother called me back the day after that. After five minutes, he was willing to help me in any way that he possibly could. This man and his wife, without knowing much at all, welcomed me back and were willing to do anything to help—unconditional love. He contacted our dad, who called me. Within days, my dad sent money to me. He had taken out a loan against the equity he had in his home—he knew it was going to be expensive and was willing to do whatever it took. It was almost Friday.

. . . . .

Seven days is a very short time in which to accept that everything could be gone, completely re-navigate a relationship that has lasted more than half of your life, learn how family court works, and come to terms with the fact that the most intimate aspects of your life are now public. All the while, you must appear unaffected. Peter was prepared: calm, cool, collected, and supported by his family, my former therapist, Stan, our oldest daughter and her boyfriend. There were very damaging affidavits and motions. One party can say anything in a motion and it is up to the other person to prove otherwise. Right from the start, Peter revealed, in great detail, the abuse that I had suffered as a child, he took real events and exaggerated them, sensationalized them. He also became extremely adept at projection, this is what it's called when a person ascribes their own feelings, thoughts and experiences to someone else. Reading his document, I said to myself, "but... that was him... not me... he did that..."

I didn't know that a child could be taken from their mother because of childhood abuse experienced by the mother. He rang every single custody bell that he could; he was prepared and had been coached.

. . . . .

I met with my attorney and we went over the documents—I needed to prepare to fight. I asked her, feeling so misunderstood and not fully comprehending the injustice of what was happening, "Doesn't anyone see that this all came after I filed an Emergency Protective Order? Isn't it obvious this is retaliation?" All she said is "I do." If not for her, I would not have my son today.

Peter had said to me, over and over: "If you ever mention domestic violence, if you ever try to leave, I will take everything from you, your children, your public respect, and it will be easy." He was right and his threats were real.

26 IT'S FRIDAY

COURT WAS A CIRCUS. PETER, once again, had all of his witnesses in order, prepared to publicly humiliate me as much as the courts would allow. I work in the field of domestic violence and, when writing papers, authors generally conclude with how to prevent abuse and violence. So why, when so many of us are spending careers writing about how to stop abuse, does it continue at such an alarming rate? Because abusers are fantastic at becoming the victim in the story and at making the victim out to be the perpetrator. It takes a perceptive, well-trained person to see the real abuser. Thankfully, in my case there were a few of these people; unfortunately, there are others who did not see him until the end.

. . . . .

Peter made three distinct accusations against me, which I had to prove were false. The snowball was rolling down the hill and it would be a great battle to stop it, and roll it back up the hill and over to the other side.

Accusation number one: mental illness, accusation number two: child abuse and number three: I had allowed underage drinking. Peter "diagnosed" me with borderline personality disorder and with multiple personality disorder.

. . . . .

Stan, about the time of our final hearing in August of 2011, was the respondent in his own case. Stan, though he settled, stated that the Kentucky Board of Examiners of Psychology—the Complainant— would prove the violations alleged in the Notice of Administrative Hearing by a preponderance of the evidence:

One count failing to maintain professional records; 2) negligent in the practice of psychology; 3) committing any misleading act or practice; and 4) failing to prepare the client appropriately for the termination.

Stan received three years of probation, he was required to undergo weekly supervision of at least two hours per week for at least one year, and obtain eighteen hours of continuing education credits in the area of boundary issues, and treatment of personality disorders.

I could file a complaint against Stan myself. He compared me to a female client, one for which he was under investigation, prior to this latest investigation, more than he counseled me. I do not think that I was like her or acted like her at all. He seemed obsessed with her and I think that he was displacing me for her and that he misdiagnosed me, based on his interaction with that other woman and Peter's assessment of me. Peter openly supported this man in the church we were attending and he opposed the woman, the two of them had a history.

Stan told me he had diagnosed most of the women in his practice with borderline personality disorder and/or multiple personality disorder—that was his area of specialty. Was he an expert who found clients with these illnesses or did he see the phantoms of these illnesses when they were not there? The month before the initial court appearance, both Peter and my oldest daughter began seeing him, which is completely unethical. I believe that this was a central piece of Peter's trap for me.

. . . . .

Sociopaths thrive on drama, chaos and refraction. They cannot spend too much time on any one point because it's so far from reality and truth. They are on to their fourth point, while the victim is still stuttering about how the first three points are lies and then, suddenly, the fourth point is fact, it is truth. The sociopath is very regulated and very in control. They are puppeteers, dictating everything so they can just sit calmly back and watch. They don't get anxious, don't flinch or waver; they look you directly in the eye and lie. Meanwhile, the perplexed, out-of-control victims become deregulated. We do feel and act "crazy" because we are being told that red is blue, but we know that red is not blue, and no one will listen. They are extremely confident about their final point being truth (after a string of other confusing points); generally, they are well dressed/groomed, poised and well-spoken, so, no one challenges them... at first.

. . . . .

My attorney encouraged me to say nothing; we had to wait for them to go through all of their antics and then, we would slowly prove otherwise. I had to willingly and publicly be re-victimized.

I sat back and allowed the abuse to run over me and through me, without saying a word; I continued to do this for more than a year. I became a stronger person—he underestimated me.

. . . . .

By 2:00 p.m. on Friday, I was allowed to have my son for three hours a day, a couple of days a week, and all day Saturday. I payed twelve hundred dollars per month in child support, along with more than one thousand dollars per month toward court-ordered therapy;

I was ordered to pay seventy percent of all ordered services for the children. The court recommended that I attend weekly therapy and a weekly alcohol abuse program, and ordered me to participate in a full-family psychological evaluation. Peter had no individual court-ordered responsibilities. Once again, I was supporting a family of five with the same job I'd held for more than a decade; I provided our health insurance, most of the Guardian Ad Litem (GAL's) fees, my therapy and attorney costs. By this time, my daughters had turned of age, and Peter was extremely underemployed; still, he was given primary time share of our children. My value and worth to my family was monetary only.

I had two friends waiting for me; I left with them in utter astonishment and in silence.

27 LET THE SPECTACLE BEGIN

AT THAT TIME I MADE approximately one hundred thousand dollars a year. Peter worked a part-time job and brought in more (of my) money than I did. I began a life that was completely foreign to me. I worked full-time as an assistant professor at one university, and taught three undergraduate classes and one graduate class at another university. I was also scheduling meetings with psychologists, the GAL and my attorney, finding it hard to simply survive each day without falling to pieces. I nearly lost my job. I got into trouble for teaching as an adjunct at the other university (the one where I had procured a part-time position for Peter). I defended myself, saying that I had overwhelming expenses trying to get a divorce. I had no idea of what I could do except work more. It took a few months for me to learn I could take out money from my retirement and when this became an option I did that instead and quit my second job. My supervisor had already begun documenting my absences.

I had no idea how to maneuver through this legal process, what to say and, more importantly, what not to say.

. . . . .

When Peter filed his first motion and the court determined that ours was a hostile situation, the children were assigned a GAL to represent their best interest. She called me for an interview. I told her that I was the victim of domestic violence and showed to her the pictures of my badly-beaten face. Not one time in that year of litigation did she mention the abuse; she dismissed it completely. I told her about a recent event—it had happened after I let Peter return after living with Charlene—where Peter had become frustrated at our son about him not eating his dinner so he picked up the medal chair he was sitting in and threw it with our son still in the chair against the wall. Peter's discipline was often like that, he would be very passive and then explode with physical abuse. I told her of another incident where Peter had choked my youngest daughter. Nothing came of any of that with the GAL. At every court appearance, she suggested that my son have less time with me and more time with his father, the abuser. She recommended hours of counseling and group work for me and required absolutely nothing of him. I was the professional, being promoted within the same organization for a decade, and my word meant nothing.

When I met with the GAL first, she had already met with Peter, so my interview was almost completely a defense of what had been said about me.

· · · · ·

Accusation number three: I had allowed under-age drinking. I was wrong to have had alcohol in my house with teenagers, especially considering how the separation and impending divorce were affecting my then sixteen- and nineteen-year-old daughters. *If I could go back, I would do it differently*; I would get rid of any alcohol and leave no questions. The GAL "recommended" that I attend a course designed for people who had been convicted of drinking and drug related offenses. I was not being ordered, but it was one of many hoops I would need to jump through. Of course I would go to "rehab."

28 IN THE BEST INTEREST OF THE CHILDREN

THE GAL HAD ARRANGED DROP offs at the children's god-parents' home (Susan and David's). The divorce was deemed so hostile that there needed to be a witness to all interactions. The plan was to drop my son off at 7:00 p.m. so that Peter could take him home for bed; he would be with me three days a week from 3:00 p.m. until 7:00 p.m. and all day on Saturdays. The GAL also reported that my son was bonded to me and did not have a bond with his father and that this was going to be traumatic for him.

Preparing for the very first drop off, my son and my younger daughter started to melt down. She was upset about the situation and angry at me, while my son was completely hysterical about leaving me. He was screaming, hiding, running away, throwing things and hitting me. I watched as he wet himself. I called Susan and said, "Peter will understand; tell him I need to change him and rock him for just ten minutes to calm him down." Susan called Peter and then called me right back. She was obviously shaken and reported that she had told him what was happening and he had responded, "that means nothing to me." She said that it was so cold and unfeeling, it sent shivers down her spine. He said that if I didn't have the children at Susan and David's house on time, he would take legal action against me. I was scared. I put my son over my shoulder and carried him to the car kicking, screaming, crying, hitting. I put him in the back seat and locked the door. At that moment, I knew that this neglect was something different; his was his own flesh and blood and he did not care. I could not appeal to a conscience; I was dealing with a sociopath.

Susan and David saw all of this and, in the months that followed, they were instrumental in keeping me above water. From time to time, they sat me down and told me to keep getting out of bed and keep fighting. I would lose "my little man" to palpable evil if I weakened or slipped into extreme emotion. I coped by turning this intense injustice into a "dissertation" for our final divorce trial. I began to compile evidence of financial abuse and created a timeline, documenting his sexual obsessions and his emotional, physical and mental abuse.

So began my new existence. Once or twice every month I spent an entire Friday in court, waiting to have Peter's latest motion heard. The motions were meant to humiliate me, break me and defeat me. Much of their content was completely unnecessary. The mental illness argument was very difficult to disprove. He had spent years establishing this "truth" about me. Utilizing his counseling degree and professional experience, he had "diagnosed me." He stated that I refused to maintain treatment throughout our marriage. This could not be further from the truth; he had required me to be in therapy, always selecting the therapists and "monitoring my progress." I, too eager to please him, had agreed and allowed him to convince me of what was wrong with me. I was so worn down after years of judgment and scrutiny; he analyzed every detail of my life, set the standard impossibly high and always shifted expectations. I was an ongoing failure. The only reason that I stopped attending therapy was that our finances would not allow it. When we did not have money for necessities, I couldn't justify spending money on therapy. Peter also criticized me for being in such need of therapy that I put the family in financial ruin. I was in a perpetual cycle of "doing what he said," only to find it used against me in another circumstance. I didn't have a self or a shred of self-confidence, self-respect or self-esteem. I did not have the ability to decide what would be best in each circumstance; I was only trying to please Peter. Now, I realize that was/is impossible; I wish I had known this earlier.

. . . . .

One night, while my son was with Peter, I was going through the things that he had left in the house. Hidden in the garage, I found his journals. His "journals" were documentation of me—hundreds and hundreds of pages. I could not believe it. He had been docu-menting me, without my knowledge, since the beginning of our re-lationship. Entries included date, time and event. An event was often something as simple as my pulling too far into an intersection while I was driving, because that is something an inexperienced teenager would do; he named this my "teenager personality." Peter documented "affairs" that I'd had with women and men that I could not even remember. In his version, I was having sex and inappro-priate relationships with nearly everyone I encountered. In these journals, he recorded emails and phone numbers that he had taken off of my phone. He recounted conversations he overheard while I was on the phone. He documented what I wore and who I inter-acted with while wearing those clothes. These journals were ency-clopedias of all of my wrongs, mostly wrongs against him, both real and imagined. It was obvious that he kept them to "prove," to "win," to "fight injustice." I felt sick and numb. Peter was obsessed with controlling and monitoring me. No wonder he couldn't work much; no wonder he so easily brought out the "black box" of my errors during arguments. No wonder I escalated; how could I com-pete? No wonder he was so prepared that first day in court.

He had successfully proven, with the best possible eye wit-nesses, that I was emotionally de-stabilized to the point of dissocia-tion. Abusers accomplish this by making the environment of someone, in my case, someone who already has post-traumatic stress disorder, unstable and unpredictable. Peter offered no safety or security, not financially or emotionally. He offered no love or commitment, he often expressed that he was "one foot in and one foot out of the relationship," and "I love you, but I'm not in love with you." Peter told me that I was worthless and that I would be alone if it were not for him. He was so financially irresponsible that I was constantly problem solving and at one point had to maintain three jobs. I felt like I could not get to solid ground, that I had no foundation, no one to count on. Of course, I was unsettled and de-stabilized. He was the exact opposite of what I needed and rightfully expected in marriage partnership, and I believe that this was his in-tention.

Though I copied those journals, thinking that I could prove his obsession (there was bizarre sexual content about his mother, as well), the GAL was not concerned about him, only about me. His unhealthy contribution to our relationship did not matter. However, I was required to attend Dialectical Behavioral Therapy (DBT) for two and a half hours every week in addition to my weekly one-hour individual therapy; my prescribed "rehab" continued. In addition to meeting these requirements, I worked full time, providing the only insurance for our entire family. I was the "crazy drunk," while taking care of a family of five.

. . . . .

Peter showed himself to be a sociopath, without conscience, well beyond the narcissist I initially thought that he was. My attorney urged me to recognize this Peter; this is who he had always been.

29 CLAIMED ABUSE VS. REAL ABUSE

PETER ACCUSED ME OF GRABBING the back of my younger daughter's head and smashing her face down onto the kitchen stove. The court-assigned social worker came to my house soon after the first divorce hearing to interview me and check the house. This social worker was half the age of the GAL and immediately saw the true nature of domestic violence in my relationship with Peter and the correlation between that dysfunction and using alcohol to self-medicate. She wondered why Peter wasn't in anger management classes. I explained the horror of the most recent few weeks and I told her about the position that the GAL had taken on our case. She recommended that I take twelve alcohol abuse classes, and that I start that Wednesday.

I let myself off of the hook. There really was an unfortunate event with my daughter, one which I very much regret, but I had not slammed her head down. That day, my daughter gave me a hard time and Peter joined in. They laughed at me and Peter told her that I did not know how to be a mother; he told her to just ignore me. They also joked about my saggy boobs, as they sometimes did. I nursed all three children; my boobs sagged. I was ashamed of my breasts, my stretch marks and my whole body. I had been used; I didn't want to nurse my first child, but we were so poor that I had no choice. Peter and my daughter were chipping away at the core of my womanhood—my sexuality and self-worth. The two people mocking me were the ones who had used my breasts, and now they were disgusted. My daughter would never have come up with this if Peter and I had been in a loving relationship; a loving partner would never have allowed her to talk to me this way, much less joined in. They both should have honored the scars of my motherhood.

In the moment, I lost control. I wish so much that I could go back in time and maintain control. My daughter yelled in my face; I wanted her to respect me and to listen to me. I took my frustration out on her inappropriately. I slammed her into the wall and I screamed in her face. I scared her; I saw terror on her face. There were other similar events with both daughters when I lost my temper.

30 REHAB CONNECTIONS

ON MY FIRST DAY OF alcohol abuse classes, I drove to a building across the street from a strip club, in a part of town that I had rarely visited. I walked into "rehab" and sat on a couch in between two college-aged young men. Directly across the room, sat a women in her fifties. At a table, sat the instructor, another woman who looked to be my age and a tattooed man in his late twenties. In a chair, sat a young lady, also in her late twenties. I introduced myself and I briefly told my story. Soon, I learned that the two young men with whom I shared a couch had been arrested for running a very successful marijuana business out of their dorm room. The woman in her fifties, a self-professing alcoholic, had just been arrested for her third DUI in less than one month. The young lady in the chair, Anna, was addicted to pills and wasn't ready to give them up yet. Jimmy, the tattooed young man, invited me to go to Florida on a prescription drug run. The woman who appeared to be my age, Sally, was a former Las Vegas stripper who had lost her daughter, as I had lost my son. She admitted that she drank, and she looked like and acted like she was on something else. Each attendee was at a different point within their court order, some finished and left, as new ones arrived. They called me "the professor" and they were all intrigued by my story, by the injustice on the "other side of the tracks." A few weeks later, Sandy walked in. She had just gotten out of jail for assaulting her partner. She worked at the same university that I did and she had hit rock bottom.

Sandy had also married an abuser when she was nineteen years old and pregnant. She and her abuser had, like Peter and I had, a second child a few years later. Abusive relationships are built on chaos, not stability. Life-changing decisions keep the victim off balance. Sandy's story was so similar to mine; she also had a third child later on in life. The main difference between us is that her abuser had abandoned her, along with her three daughters when she moved in with a new partner, a woman in her twenties. Sandy's relationship with her new partner was volatile when they were drinking. One evening, things got out of control. They ended up in an altercation and Sandy's partner called the police. The police arrested Sandy on an alcohol charge and on assault. Because no father was in the picture, Sandy's mother was called to care for the children. This was Sandy's first experience with law enforcement and neither she nor her mother had any idea what would happen next. Her mother called the jail and told them that Sandy must be suicidal; this must be the answer to her behavior. Sandy had always been "a good girl and never been in trouble." Sandy was immediately stripped and taken to the suicide watch area. She was put in what inmates call "The Turtle Suit," the same thing that patients wear when they receive an X-Ray. It's a hard shield-like cover; the patient is naked underneath it, and it is very cold inside the jail cell. Sandy was in her Turtle Suit for three days. After the first day, she was allowed a phone call; she called her mother, desperately begging her mother to stop saying that she was suicidal, trying to explain to her the consequences. Her mother did not relent. Sandy couldn't cry—crying led to more time under suicide watch. The inmate "watchers" whispered this to her: "don't cry or get mad, or they'll leave you in here." Three days later, she finally convinced her mother that she was not suicidal and she was able to get out of jail.

Anna, who had been assigned to suicide watch during her thirty-day stretch in jail, chimed in while Sandy talked, affirming Sandy's terrible recounting of Turtle Suit treatment.

Sandy was "in the system." Her children were assigned to a GAL, and their GAL decided that it was a good idea to have her nineteen-year-old daughter become the guardian of the younger two girls. Sandy was allowed visitation with her younger two daughters, as I was with my son. In a matter of just a few weeks, her daughters had become uncontrollable. Everyone at Sandy's work found out, and, because she was a professional in the medical field, the story was scandalous. Sandy had difficulty making ends meet, considering all of the legal bills. She returned to jail, for two more weekends, to serve out her time. She learned from others in the class to dress warmly and stuff dollar bills in her socks, to just sit there, not talk much and do her time.

Anna, a young, attractive, smart woman, who had so much going for her, had almost overdosed the week before this group meeting. The instructor tried to convince her to enter a treatment program, but she was not ready to give up the pills. Anna reported, weeks later, that when she had been pulled over with some college friends, loaded up with dope, she hadn't cared.

31 COURT-ORDERED THERAPY

WHILE WRITING A PAPER FOR work, I came across an interesting journal article that articulated my plight, Abused Mothers' Safety Concerns and Court Mediators' Custody Recommendations. In the article Intimate Partner Violence (IPV) is defined as:

"A pattern of coercive control that may be primarily made up of psychological abuse, sexual coercion, or economic abuse, that is punctuated by one or more acts of frightening physical violence, credible threat of physical harm, or sexual assault."

"Along with the damaging effects of physical abuse on women's health and well-being, emotional abuse appears to be even more deleterious, and also tends to occur more frequently than physical or sexual violence. Emotional abuse includes harassment, controlling and isolating behaviors, and destruction of property, degradation, humiliation, threats, and insults. Survivors of IPV often report that the emotional abuse was worse than the physical violence. Emotional

abuse has been found to predict poor mental health outcomes such as depression, higher levels of stress and/or Post Traumatic Stress Disorder, and low self-esteem over and above physical abuse."

"Although many victimized women end their relationships with the expectation that the abuse will end as well, batterers often continue, or even escalate, their abuse post-separation. Much of this abuse is directed at and/or involves the manipulation of shared children."

"Abusers often perform well under observation and manipulate mediators [and court professionals] ....thus are viewed more favorably than the victims."

"Mothers who disclosed the domestic violence were more likely to have their concerns ignored, lose custody, receive unsafe custody exchange recommendations.."

" Most of the mothers had serious concerns about the children's emotional well-being. Several described the fathers' exceptional ability to manipulate others—including the children. Attempting to turn children against their mothers, some fathers told the children that the mothers were to blame for the divorce, were tearing the family apart, and/or were mentally unstable....discussing too many details of the divorce and custody battle with children.."

"Most women in the study suffered abuse that was more controlling or emotional—types of abuse that are extremely difficult, if not impossible, to document...court professionals require documentation...several women described that the courts view physical abuse as the only legitimate form of abuse.."

"The women had a variety of concerns at the time of mediation: 1) the father's previous and likely ongoing emotional abuse of the children 2) losing the children to him due to kidnapping or alienation, and/or 3) the father's inability to provide a stable environment for the children. In other words, women had

legitimate concerns that deserved to be taken seriously, however their concerns were rarely considered [11]."

. . . . .

Neither the GAL, nor the therapist assigned to the children brought up any of Peter's abuse against me during the year in court. The GAL consistently turned conversations to accusations of my promiscuity and to my emotional affair. She had very little training, if any. In the end, she actually documented that my son was manipulative and that he was creating all of the confusion.

. . . . .

I recently checked the GAL's professional website; two of her areas of legal specialty are custody and domestic violence.

. . . . .

The court-ordered child therapist, Amy, did not consider that Peter and the rest of the Waltons might have fed lies to the girls; they were re-writing history. Amy also suggested that my son was causing the problems. She regularly communicated with the GAL and was the one who planted the idea in the GAL's mind. My then-minor daughter's "therapy" focused solely on my mental illness. Neither the therapist, nor the GAL considered that my youngest daughter

152

had acknowledged that the best recent time in her relationship with me was the many-month stretch when Peter was living with a female subordinate of his.

. . . . .

Amy did not consider Adverse Childhood Events (ACEs) as anything other than a problem, which left me with the burden of trying to prove why the court should not abate my parental rights. I was not asked "what happened to you?" only told, "calm down, you are out of control." The official approach to me was not, "how can I help you be a better parent?" but rather, "I am advising taking your normal parental rights, because of your abuse and your behavior, until you prove otherwise. And calm down."

We had a full family evaluation. Peter's results were "too perfect;" therefore the results inconclusive and invalid. Sociopaths are often "too perfect." The director of the center gave me a fairly good evaluation, but his assistant, Lynn, ruined any chance that I had to restore a relationship with my youngest daughter. Lynn had taken Stan's diagnoses of me and highlighted them in the report, which became the basis for Amy's therapy with my younger daughter. Lynn did not listen to any of my concerns. Instead, she saw them as paranoid and saw me as unfit. When I tried to show her evidence based studies validating my case, she did not acknowledge the documents, she just left them sitting on the table in front of us. All of my fears eventually came to fruition, right down to my son eating a lot of chocolate, then not brushing his teeth while he was with Peter and, consequently, having to have several teeth pulled. So many of his teeth were pulled that he had to have a bracket put in his mouth to keep space for his permanent teeth. Lynn stated that I was promiscuous and she downplayed any positive interaction that I had with my children while under her observation. Later, when confronted, she admitted to my court-ordered therapist that she came to her conclusions about me, based on Peter's input. Peter would regularly quote from Lynn's report up until communication with him ended.

Both the GAL and the children's therapist, Amy, talked to me in very condescending ways, even when I attempted to show scientific literature backing my case; both were nothing more than patronizing. It was very difficult to not express emotion when I was losing my children. Adding to my stress, the financial burden was increasing exponentially every week and it rested almost solely on my shoulders. Neither my attorney nor my therapists had ever seen a GAL bill so much; GALs generally try to keep costs down, aware that parents are already paying attorney fees. The GAL did not seem to be aware that her role was supposed to be one of altruism, of helping children.

. . . . .

No one mentioned the photos or the abuse. When my sessions followed Peter's, it was obvious that he spent most of the interview and session time talking negatively about me. This meant that I had

154

to spend much of my time defending myself. This lack of voice triggered me, making me look crazier. No one considered the effects of the abusive relationship: the consequences to my mental health, the drinking or my impaired relationship with the girls. No one mentioned Peter's girlfriend, Charlene, or the fact that he lived with her while I was pregnant. No one brought up the fact that I had been the family breadwinner, taking care of our three children and of Peter, himself. There were so many red flags and there was so much literature available to these women; the abuse and Parent Alienation Syndrome so obvious. When teenage girls turn 100% on their mother, cannot think of any positive thing that their mother has offered to them in their entire lives, take care of the emotional needs of their father, make fun of "mental illnesses," make outlandish accusations against their mother and say nothing negative about their father, how are abused women supposed to get away, without leaving children with a perpetrator?

32

AMY: THE CHILDREN'S COURT-

ORDERED THERAPIST

IN THE SUMMER OF 2010, when Peter finally left, I did not know what was happening with my daughters, so I sought the advice of a psychologist colleague; a well-published researcher in child abuse prevention. He introduced me to something called Parent Alienation Syndrome (PAS) and he recommended another expert, a colleague of his. I called this expert immediately and she agreed that I was experiencing PAS. Because the PAS was already well underway, Peter had enough ammunition to call my parenting into question; a lazy man who was unwilling to work was seen as the primary caregiver and superior parent. Tellingly, our youngest child, the one whose response was most genuine, showed a clear bond with me and not with Peter. As part of a court order, I was required to attend weekly therapy with a mutually-agreed-upon therapist, as were both

minor children. In 2010, Peter did not know that he agreed to someone with whom I had already spoken, the recommended expert. I
thought that I was finally catching a break.

When I brought our first encounter up with the therapist/"expert," she denied everything, including her experience with PAS.

. . . . .

After a simple internet search, I identified with nearly every description of PAS.

What is PAS?

Gardner, author of *The Parent Alienation Syndrome*, defines PAS
as:

"1. *The PAS is a disorder that arises primarily in the context of child-
    custody disputes.*

2. *Its primary manifestation is the child's campaign of denigration against
    a parent, a campaign that has no justification.*

3. *It results from the combination of a programming (brainwashing) of a
    parent's indoctrinations and the child's own contributions to the vilifi-
    cation of the targeted parent."*

What is the child's part in PAS?

Gardner notes that the PAS is more than brainwashing or programming, because the child has to actually participate in the deni-
grating of the alienated parent. This is done in primarily the
following eight ways:

"1. The child denigrates the alienated parent with foul language and severe oppositional behavior.

2. The child offers weak, absurd, or frivolous reasons for his or her anger.

3. The child is sure of himself or herself and doesn't demonstrate ambivalence, i.e. love and hate for the alienated parent, only hate.

4. The child exhorts that he or she alone came up with ideas of denigration. The "independent-thinker" phenomenon is where the child asserts that no one told him to do this.

5. The child supports and feels a need to protect the alienating parent.

6. The child does not demonstrate guilt over cruelty towards the alienated parent.

7. The child uses borrowed scenarios, or vividly describes situations that he or she could not have experienced.

8. Animosity is spread to the friends and/or extended family of the alienated parent."

"In severe cases of parent alienation, the child is utterly brain- washed against the alienated parent. The alienator can truthfully say that the child doesn't want to spend any time with this parent, even though he or she has told him that he has to, it is a court order, etc. The alienator typically responds, 'There isn't anything that I can do about it. I'm not telling him that he can't see you' [12]."

. . . . .

Amy recommended that I not see my then-sixteen-year-old daughter. Amy suggested to my daughter that she read a book about borderline personality disorder, and my daughter frequently quoted from the book to me. Visitation was very difficult with my daughter; she expressed Peter's stance so articulately that she sounded just like him. She pushed my buttons. No one helped things to get better. No one helped her, no one helped me and no one helped our relationship. The professionals remained focused on my mental health problems, exactly as Peter had orchestrated.

Contrary to Lynn's recommendations, the director of the center (Lynn's supervisor) led our evaluation and recommended that visits continue. This director asserted our teenage daughter should be told that adult topics wouldn't be addressed with her until she was an adult. This needed to be shut down. Amy's, Lynn's and the GAL's voices were louder.

Our younger daughter was a victim in what psychological literature calls emotional incest; another thing that both Amy and Lynn failed to identify. Our teenager had taken my place as Peter's partner, so she became increasingly isolated; her friend group dwindled.

. . . . .

After the divorce trial concluded, Amy finally admitted to me that Peter leaned on my daughter; our teenager had disclosed to Amy that she felt as though she needed to take care of Peter, that he was the victim in the divorce and Amy said that, in her opinion Peter was "a very sick man." It took more than a year and a half for Amy to be forthright about Peter. She and Lynn further damaged my re-

lationship with my daughter at the time that they had the opportunity to actually assist in healing and helping. During our final therapy session, Amy spent most of our time telling me about a client
of hers who was experiencing severe PAS and she asked me if I
knew anyone that could help him. I thought I might be in the *Twi-
light Zone.* Amy was extremely weak, unwilling to take a stand on my
behalf (even after Peter had been identified as the perpetrator), or
she was uninformed/uneducated (and, therefore, should not have
been practicing), or she intended to hurt me (and, therefore, should
not have been practicing).

33 COURT-ORDERED DBT

AFTER EVERY ACCUSATION THAT PETER made, I had to dispute it by fulfilling the orders of the court. Judges have to rule on many cases in such a short amount of time, that they rely heavily on the professionals involved in the cases, on their observations, opinions and expertise. Because the GAL, Amy and Lynn opposed me and believed all of Peter's accusations, the Judge required me to go through treatment before custody could be resolved. I was ordered to attend a year of DBT.

. . . . .

The DBT leaders were fantastic and I ended up getting a lot out of the curriculum. One leader agreed, within a short time of hearing my story, that Peter was a sociopath. She recommended reading materials, guided me through my own behavior changes and counseled me on how to maneuver around Peter's abuse. I have ACEs and PTSD from childhood, so the therapy benefited me. Instead of seeing me as the problem and questioning my parenting, this therapist helped me to be a better parent and person; she helped in my recovery from childhood abuse and taught to me the skills I needed to stay on track. This is the first therapist/counselor that really helped me and, interestingly, she is the only one that Peter and/or his family did not "recommend (insist upon)." She did not and does not want to be identified as supporting me; she sees Peter for who he really is and she knows that he would have no problem wreaking havoc in her life and her practice as punishment for this support. I still think very fondly of her and of what she does for those with PTSD, and I will not forget any of what she did for me or what she taught to me.

Most of the other group members were there voluntarily. They were interested and supportive, hardly believing what was happening in my life. They had self-professed issues and engaged in self-destructive behaviors; they were hurting and wanting to get better, but they didn't know how. I found that all of them were honest, vulnerable, open, endlessly supportive and sensitive to the pain of others. To this day, I have the support of the ladies from this group.

. . . . .

One woman who did not seem to need to be in the group, but had admitted herself, befriended me outside of the group. She started attending the group very shortly before I finished, so I didn't know her well in that setting. Years later, she initiated a series of events that took me right back, bringing all of the players in this story back into my life. Because this took place years after the trial, I'm saving the details of her story for my third book.

34 COURT-ORDERED INDIVIDUAL THERAPY

PETER ACCUSED ME OF NOT following through with individual therapy, thereby leaving unresolved the effects of the abuse that I endured as a child. I was ordered to attend weekly individual counseling with a court-appointed therapist. Again, this cost was out-of-pocket. At this point, the stars finally started to align in my favor. Peter did not agree to any of the therapists that I put forth, so the court ordered someone that neither of us knew. My therapist was a mediator in my Judge's courtroom and she saw Peter for who he really was, just as the DBT therapist had. She was a true help in my life that year and in the years to follow. In the end, she testified in my favor, describing me as someone enduring years of emotional, psychological and physical abuse from Peter, not just during my childhood. She advocated for me with the GAL and with the other court-appointed therapists, and, most importantly, she supported my relationship with Steven. She was key in turning the snowball in the other direction, all the while, helping me to live and to deal with unimaginable stress; she united with my attorney to battle not only Peter, but also the misguided professionals completely taken in by his sociopathy.

35

MY HEROES WERE THREE WOMEN: two psychologists and my gifted attorney. They all quickly validated the abuse that I had received, saw Peter as a sociopath, recognized the PAS and guided me through this horrible situation.

I desperately wanted my attorney, Robin, to bring the "evidence of abuse" to the table. She told me that Peter's attorney had a reputation of initiating a great deal of litigation during divorces, but losing at trial. Robin told me that colleagues had heard him bragging that the Waltons were paying his salary for the year. Robin counseled that it would be best if we only defended; we would not initiate or bring anything up until the end. Their accusations and motions would lose their power after being heard over and over. In the end, my side of the story would be shockingly fresh in the Judge's mind as it came time for final ruling. She only exposed me to the motions for which she needed my help in responding. She represented me by handling Peter, the GAL and Peter's attorney, only allowing me to be in the same room with Peter when it was absolutely necessary. She said that I was being re-victimized, Peter was a scary individual and the GALs outright, often irrational, support of him angered her more than anything.

This reduced my triggers (I wasn't made aware of even half of what he was saying about me); I was able to sit in the courtroom and observe how our Judge ruled. He was very conservative and espoused co-parenting, joint custody, getting along, being humble, following through with any and all therapeutic suggestions and orders—overall compliance. He seemed to rule in favor of women when they were professional and well-groomed, and when they avoided emotional expression and argument. I sat in the courtroom and graded papers, etc. so that he could see that I was responsible— not a crazy disheveled drunk, but, instead, a professional woman with a lot of work to do. Peter, underemployed, argued in the next room. Peter was fighting for exactly what the Judge ruled against. All I had to do was ask for joint custody, try to participate in co-parenting, state that I thought that it was in my son's best interest to have Peter involved in his life and, above all else, show no emotion. Peter's anger would eventually come out; he would challenge the Judge's authority, eventually. And he did reveal himself in the end. Only the GAL, never saw him for who he was.

36 STEVEN AND ME

STEVEN AND I COMMUNICATED DAILY after I re-initiated contact. After a few weeks of constant communication, he sent an email to me from his work account. It was a military email; I looked up his location and found a Navy SEAL base close to his home. I asked him if he was a SEAL and he said, "Yes," with a chuckle. This increased my attraction to him. I was captivated by him and the mountaineering gig, but this created in me a whole new level of respect for him. He said that he didn't want me to know until he knew that I was interested him, as a person, so that he could be certain that I wasn't simply caught up in what he did for a living. His ex-wife married him because he was a SEAL—this was not going to happen again.

. . . . .

We planned our first rendezvous for September. He planned to come home to his dad and stepmother's house, which was six hours from me, for a visit. I taught a class on terrorism and disasters. He would guest lecture, giving him an excuse to be in town. He told his dad about us and about why he would be leaving for a few days. I told Peter that I was on a work trip for a few days. Steven reserved a hotel room halfway between my home and his dad's. When I walked through the door, he grabbed me, lifted me up against the wall... it was the best sex we had ever had. He had everything planned, so we didn't have to leave at all. I experienced sensations that I had never felt before, over and over.

Our first real date was in a hotel room. It was passionate, but it confused the whole dating process. We were so advanced in some aspects of our relationship and just beginning in others. Steven and I took our relationship one trip at a time. We both were all in, but wouldn't cling if it fizzled. We weren't forcing it; if it was meant to be, it would all work out. Every time he was in the lower forty-eight, I met him and sometimes he came directly to me. That first year, we saw each other every three months or so. We now refer to this time as "the dirty days."

· · · · ·

During one visit, Steven invited his dad and stepmother to meet us halfway, at the hotel where he and I had stayed at in September, in order to meet me. We all got along remarkably well. When I met his dad, I knew that if Steven turned out like his father, I had hit the jackpot. Steven's dad was so kind, gentle and loving, and I observed the loving, sweet relationship that he enjoyed with Steven's step-mother. After I met them, I was even more enamored with Steven. We all had a fabulous time together.

37 THE FAMILY THAT STOLE THANKSGIVING

November 2010

PETER AND I DID NOT drink much in our twenties—neither coffee, nor alcohol. By our early thirties, though, both alcohol and coffee became more regular parts of our lives. I started abusing alcohol in my mid-thirties and I escalated to an astonishing level at times, especially between the time that I let Peter back in the house in 2009 and the start of our divorce. I drank to escape. I drank in order to sleep. It wasn't really the amount of alcohol, it was the speed that I drank, right before bedtime. I got sober as soon as I was served that first motion—primarily out of fear.

. . . . .

Shortly after divorce proceedings started, I gave a phone to my son. This way, he could be more in control of communication and could text me or call me freely. My brother and his family spent Thanksgiving with me so that I wouldn't be alone and so that my son could play with his cousins.

I was adding my brother and sister-in-law's phone numbers into this phone when I found naked pictures of my son. Shaking and scared, I showed them to my sister-in-law. I was helpless. I could not protect my son.

. . . . .

My son innocently relayed stories of Ben, Mary Ellen and Peter drinking heavily and, without knowing what he was doing, described himself as unsupervised and unprotected. Ben and Mary Ellen had a son, Sean, who was younger than my son, but bigger, aggressive and demanding. My son, traumatized by the divorce, was in a weakened state—introverted, insecure and easily dominated. He was clearly afraid of Sean. The two boys were left alone, for hours, to play. My son periodically called me from the bathroom, crying and saying that he was hiding, trying to get away from Sean. I asked him if he told Peter or Ben or Mary Ellen; he said that he had, but that they had dismissed him and did not investigate the "play time" or environment. "Play time" lasted until after 11:00 pm on school nights. He said that Sean would regularly follow him into the bathroom to try and touch his penis. My son tried to lock himself in the bathroom, sometimes successfully, because he wanted to get away from Sean. My son experienced unwanted touch and this was documented in our family evaluation. Sean molested my son on Peter's watch.

I called a friend of mine, who was on the police force, and he advised me to immediately call 911. The police officer took this very seriously. He confiscated the phone and took it to the cyber-crimes unit, and a detective was assigned to the case.

I had to send my son back to Peter's the next day, as Peter had him for the weekend. This was a devastating and sickening moment in my life. David and Susan's son and daughter-in-law were visiting the drop off house. When Peter arrived, Sean was with him. David and Susan's son and daughter-in-law observed my son, scared and anxious, not wanting to leave with Peter. In desperation, I called my oldest daughter and pled with her to look after her brother—maybe even take care of him. She laughed and hung up.

. . . . .

By Monday, the investigation was in full force. The police interviewed Ben, Mary Ellen, Peter, Sean and my son. My attorney called an emergency hearing (the only time we acted offensively) for that Wednesday. The Judge, very concerned, expressed his view. The GAL said that "the mother is over-reacting. This is a case of boys being boys. I recommend less time with the mother because she is psychologically damaging the boy." My attorney later told me that the court professionals in the room could not believe that a GAL would not advise protection of the child, at least until the investigation concluded, when there was a question of sexual abuse and lack of supervision. The GAL recommended that the phone be taken from my son and that all of his interactions be supervised by the other parent, by Peter. She stripped my son of the ability to ask for help and of the ability to control the situation with Peter. The Judge ruled against the GAL and Peter, and ordered that my son was not allowed to be in the presence of Sean for any reason and under any circumstance. The Judge took the situation very seriously.

. . . . .

Again, I had developed maladaptive coping skills and could not figure out how to deal with a situation that was completely out of my control. I could not protect my child; he was scared and he often wet or soiled himself in his pants when it was time to leave me and go back to Peter's house. The GAL actually recommended that I have less time with my son because I was overreacting to what, in her words, was simply a matter of "boys will be boys." This was too much. I couldn't figure out how to handle my emotions. That night I attended my rehab group. I was glad to not be alone and to have support, but when it was time to go home, I was overwhelmed with loneliness and helplessness. My poor son, my daughter's response to me... I stopped for several bottles of wine and some vodka.

38 ME AND SALLY THE STRIPPER

I MET SALLY AT MY recommended "rehab" group. She had a similar story to mine and she offered to me understanding and support. During the meeting immediately after the special court hearing about my son, I took up most of the group's time relaying the day's events and, specifically, how the GAL obviously opposed my being with my son. To say I was undone would be an understatement. That weekend, my son was with Peter; because of the GAL, Peter maintained his time share. Friday night, while I was in my bed, watching television and ready for sleep, I got a call from Sally. She was concerned about me and offered to take me out for the night— she thought that it would be good for me. She, a former stripper, knew several strippers in town and wanted to take me to where they worked. I was curious; I wondered what strip clubs were like, what the men in my life had experienced at them. Peter encouraged sexual deviance, but when I engaged in it, he responded with unbridled, unending emotional and psychological abuse. Then, Peter used my behavior as an excuse to behave badly, himself. Steven was also encouraging me to try new things and he wanted me to go to the strip club. I knew that it was not a good idea; I should've stayed in my bed, but I rationalized the decision, so I got up and prepared for a night out on the town.

I called a male friend of mine and asked him if he would be the designated driver for the night. He agreed to drive us and to take us to some of his own favorite places.

First, we went to a piano bar where I had two vodka tonics within an hour. Then we went to a local strip club that Sally recommended. I drank more vodka tonics and some wine. I had lost a significant amount of weight and had not been drinking for quite some time, so I became very intoxicated, very quickly.

We stayed until the place shut down, at which point, my friend had to carry me to his vehicle. As he buckled me in, I realized that I had left my cell phone in the club. He went back inside to retrieve my phone, leaving the running vehicle parked at the front entrance. As soon as he went in to the club, Sally started panicking, saying that he wanted a threesome and that we should take his vehicle and get away from him. Sally, who had been in the back seat, suddenly appeared in the front seat. She drove for a couple of feet before bumping into a taxi cab. I was so drunk that I don't really know what happened next; she was just gone.

The taxi driver unbuckled me and moved me to the driver's seat. When the police arrived, I got up and ran; my first reaction was always to run. One police officer tackled me and brought me back to the scene. By then, my friend had come out of the club, wondering what was happening. He told the officers that he left for just a few minutes and that he had buckled me in, on the passenger's side. He had no idea how I ended up in the driver's seat. The police officer cuffed me, pushed me down—hard—on the hood of the police cruiser, like they do on *COPS*, and threw me into the back. I was so scared, confined in the back of the police cruiser. When we arrived at the drunk tank, I was harshly thrown in to join those that were already there. I did not know what would happen; this was my first time getting into trouble, ever in my life. I had never had detention or been written up in school.

I tried to ask what would happen to me and what I needed to do to get help; I was met with silence. I looked up the number for the front desk at the jail and I called it. The woman who answered looked over at me, shocked, and dismissed my questions. I kept calling her, over and over. I was taken to isolation and my phone was confiscated. They breathalyzed me a second time and I blew a 0.2. The officers laughed to each other, saying that they couldn't believe that I was still standing and coherent.

They took me out of holding and booked me. When a man issued the green suit to me, he asked me how long I had worked there [at the strip club]. A female officer strip-searched me; she instructed me to bend over and cough, so I stayed bent over, not knowing when to move. She had left and when she came back in, she laughed and said that I could stand up and get dressed. She took me to isolation where I cried and paced the cell. I was supposed to get my son on Sunday and no one knew where I was.

The next day, Saturday, in the afternoon, I was taken to the same place that I had been strip-searched. I was given back my clothes and belongings. After I dressed, I was taken to the waiting room where I saw my best friend, the one who had advised me to leave Peter, who had sat in the courtroom with me, who had walked me to my car after court appearances, who regularly stayed with me when she was worried about my safety. There she sat, looking at me with love and sadness. She had paid my bail. She hugged me and we went to the car. Steven called her in the early morning hours, after I suddenly stopped communicating. He was worried and at a loss, four thousand miles away. My friend, Coco, called hospitals, morgues, coroners and, lastly, the jail. She arrived at the courthouse first thing in the morning to get me out.

. . . . .

At the moment when things might have turned in my favor, I messed up. In a few hours, I had disappointed everyone that I cared about, the people who supported me, loved me and defended me.

. . . . .

When Coco and I got to my house, we found that someone had been in my house after I had left. A roast that I had left in the crock-pot had been eaten; dirty dishes were all over the kitchen. There were women's clothes strewn through the house. It didn't look like anything had been stolen, except about four hundred dollars in cash. It was such a disturbing scene that Coco decided to stay with me until the locksmith changed all of the locks. We sat on the couch and she held me while I cried. No one had ever done that for me. She made me call my attorney; I didn't want to. My attorney meant a great deal to me and had become very important to me through the months of Peter's courtroom attacks. She was obviously disappointed and didn't know, immediately, how she would handle things; there was some time before I had to appear in court. We all hoped that no one saw my arrest report or mug shot that weekend. My attorney didn't abandon me; no one did.

When Coco left, I Skyped with Steven. He would not let me fall asleep or hide from what had happened. He made me stay awake, stay sober, deal with what happened and face the coming consequences. He wanted me to face it, head on. This was the worst trouble I had ever been in, and my son's wellbeing was at stake. I had worked so hard to do everything that the court ordered. Suddenly, I could lose it all, and I would've deserved to.

. . . . .

Only the leader of the "rehab" group noticed my arrest and jail time. I came to group, contrite and ashamed. She told me that relapses happen most often in times of acute stress; she had faith that I would stay sober this time and that I had learned my lesson. Peter had not found out so….life picked up where I had left it…

39 BACK TO THE COURTROOM

SOON AFTER THE JUDGE ORDERED Peter to keep my son away from Sean, my son started talking about Sean again. I told this to my attorney and she said that Peter could be in contempt of court; he could be put in jail. Robin called the GAL and told her that my son had been in contact with Sean. Robin set up an appointment for the GAL to interview him and document any interactions with Sean. My son did not want to go to the GAL's office, which was forty-five minutes away. The GAL did not appear to have any experience in interviewing a child about traumatic events; all of her interviews did further damage to him. By the time we got to her office, my son had wet his pants. I took him into her office, as he was, and I told her what happened. My attorney followed up after the interview and the GAL said to her, "he said nothing about seeing Sean." My attorney asked if she had asked about Sean, and she said, "no, I wanted to wait and see if he brought it up. If it was important, he would've brought it up. We just colored together."

. . . . .

Before we went back to court, we finally caught a break. Peter had boldly gone out to dinner with Ben, Mary Ellen, Sean and my son. My son relayed this information to me. My attorney found out that the restaurant had a camera system.

When we got back to court, Robin called Peter out on this dinner. The GAL defended Peter. My attorney pointed out to me that her bias was so obvious, she was even sitting with Peter and his attorney at their table.

The Judge was visibly angry at Peter as Peter explained that he didn't think the boys should be punished any longer because I was overreacting. Peter thought that it was best for my son to interact with Sean and his family. Peter was "telling" the Judge that he knew better, that the Judge's order meant nothing. The Judge asked why he shouldn't send Peter to jail right then for being in contempt. He fined Peter and ordered him to pay all attorney expenses.

40 BACKGROUND ON STEVEN AND JO

STEVEN, HIS EX-WIFE AND his family played a considerable role in my life during the year of legal proceedings, and even more in the years that followed. Before I introduce more of my story, I'm providing some of his story, for context.

· · · · ·

Jo and Steven knew each other for only a few months before marrying, something Steven regrets. When they met, he was stationed in Hawaii and she was a senior in college. At the start of summer 2004, after enduring years of verbal, mental and physical abuse, Steven decided to end his marriage to Jo; he left. The marriage was really over at this point; their remaining years together were based solely on coercion. Jo stated that if he did not come back to her, she would take his children as far away as possible and not let him see them; she threatened to ruin his career and to ruin him financially. Who would the courts believe: a damaged warrior, or a loving mother that had sacrificed her own needs to take care of the kids and the home while he was away? She was unwilling to work, which left Steven to be the sole provider, deploying continually. He had no choice, in his mind, but to return to her. By the end of that summer, he moved back in with her. This way of returning to the marriage, under threat, gave her power and control, which she exercised; her psychological and verbal abuse escalated toward Steven and toward the children.

. . . . .

In January 2009, just prior to his final overseas trip in support of the Global War on Terrorism, Jo yelled at Steven, "I hope you don't make it back from this trip!" He asked, "you want me to die?" Jo asked him to increase his life insurance policy to one and a half million dollars, antagonized him with threats, started arguments to unsettle him and to leave him vulnerable, right before engaging in life-threatening operations.

In the summer of 2009, giving his marriage one last try for the sake of his children, Steven moved his family. He had taken a position in Alaska, one that did not require deployment, which would allow the family to spend time together. The trip out to Alaska was the longest continuous time he had ever spent with Jo, and he could not endure her abuse any longer. By the end of the trip, he had contacted an attorney to file for divorce as soon as possible, after the mandated six-month waiting period. Six months later, in January 2010, Steven asked for a marriage dissolution, retaining a Judge Advocate General (JAG, military attorney) in order to keep legal fees to a minimum. In February, before leaving for a trip, Steven gave the completed paperwork to Jo. She said, "this is not how it is going to happen."

. . . . .

When Steven returned home from the trip, Jo was highly escalated and acting strangely—she was making aggressive eye contact, and staring at him continually. She had been drinking the night of his return; Steven had decided to not drink anymore following his request to dissolve the marriage, so that she could not use it against him. Jo demanded that Steven look at retirement calculations in a book about divorcing in the military. She put the book in his face, then hid it behind her back and started toward the stairs—ignoring him when he asked her to see it. Steven followed her asking to look at the book. As she turned a coroner at the base of the stairs Steven tried to smack her on the butt to get her attention. He reached around the wall separating the stairs from the downstairs, his forearm caught on the wall so he barely touched her buttock. She continued up the stairs so Steven sat back down on the couch to watch the Olympics, recovering from his training trip. She went into the room where the children were playing, and started to become hysterical, involving them. He went up to the room to check on her and he asked about the book; she responded so irrationally and emotionally, that he thought it was best to leave her alone.

The next day, Jo seemed fine. She and Steven did not talk about the previous evening, she did not show any fear of Steven and she engaged in her regular routine. He saw her getting ready and she did not have any bruises or marks on her body. She did not complain of any injury. When Steven went to work, he was served a Protective Order. Local authorities escorted him out of the building, where he was the Senior Enlisted Advisor, and back to his home. They instructed him to get his things; he would not be allowed to return home or see his children until further notice. Jo accused him of beating her the night before.

. . . . .

If this accusation had been substantiated, Steven would have been dishonorably discharged, unable to carry a firearm. The case was never investigated. During their divorce proceedings, Jo stated several times "this can all go away if you [Steven] come back to me." Because of this unsubstantiated accusation and because Alaska lagged behind the rest of the country in understanding of psychological issues, Jo was given sole custody of the children, which gave her even more power and control. She followed through on her threat, taking the children to Florida. Any time that Steven was in the area where they lived, Jo could again make false allegations; he could not go near his children for fear of her false claims.

. . . . .

Jo opposed any sort of therapy for her or for the boys. The few times that she saw a therapist, Steven believes that it was in order to document her false domestic violence accusations. This is the only time that Jo "sought help," coincidentally right at the time of her accusations. Jo created roadblocks to every attempt of Steven's to provide professional help to his boys, during the difficult divorce. The court's initial order was that he only see his sons for a few hours a day, under the condition he take them to see a professional while visiting for Christmas break 2010; Jo even tried to sabotage this. Jo refused to allow the boys to participate in the court-ordered therapy with the therapist that Steven selected, and she refused to participate, herself. After he left, she found a different therapist for the boys, but only took them a few times. Because Jo had sole custody, she had control; therapists were not able to meet with the boys without her consent, something she would not give.

. . . . .

Between 2003 and 2009 Steven noticed that Jo's verbal and physical abuse against his sons was escalating and increasing in frequency. Former friends of hers had seen this, and they later filed affidavits.

Steven's dad and stepmother had also seen Jo's deteriorating behavior. Steven's dad and stepmother commented that they overheard her harshness toward the oldest child while he was doing his homework. They had also commented on how she verbally abused Steven, right in front of them. Jo yelled and screamed a lot. According to Steven's mother, during a visit with the boys (sometime after the divorce), Jo screamed at the boys quite frequently. Throughout the boy's lives, Jo made them promise "to never leave her." On many occasions, Steven observed Jo yelling at the boys until they cried, and even witnessed her slap them in the face.

41 ROSS, BETSY AND JO

STEVEN WAS AT HIS DAD and stepmother's house for the Christmas holiday season and we planned to see each other as much as possible. My son and I celebrated Christmas day alone. I made the best of it, but it was sad and lonely for us. On Christmas afternoon, Peter and I exchanged my son and I left town to go see Steven. I was so happy to be with Steven, some of the only joy I felt in those days. I walked into the house and the first thing I saw was a gigantic picture of the family, including Jo. I also saw many pictures of Steven, Jo, and the children, and even some of Steven and Jo's wedding. It was uncomfortable, but Steven's dad and stepmother were as kind to me as they had been during our first encounter. Everything was still really good with them. Steven's biological mother seemed supportive; she had changed the photos in her home to ones of Steven and me. She told me that I had made her son smile again.

· · · · ·

Betsy and Jo were sisters-in-law for twelve years and they continued to send sister-in-law well wishes over Facebook, long after the divorce. Steven has only one brother. They never lived near each other, so their communication was generally by phone and email. Jo had nothing good to say about anyone behind their back—especially about her husband. She escalated to fever-pitched disparagement after Steven filed for divorce.

I was with Steven when he received a hostile email from Betsy, chastising him and defending Jo. Steven agonized over his response, hoping that she could hear his story. He asked Betsy to not communicate with Jo, as he had recently litigated one of Jo's motions with information that had come directly from Betsy and Ross. Jo had also quoted them within another motion, and again during their final trial, as a way of backing her allegations against Steven: "Even Steven's family, Ross and Besty…"

· · · · ·

Date: Thu, Oct 28, 2010 at 3:46 PM
Subject: Re: Bear

.....How's everything else? Are you off work for a little while? Betsy talked to Jo the other day and sounds like they are in Florida now. She's trying to figure out what to do with her life ...now. Well I hope you are alright and you are happier. I'm sure you miss the boys.

Ross

....hope the divorce gets over for you.. I can't imagine going through that. I'm sure it brings out the worst. I've been thinking I should give Thomas and Jay a call to let them know I'm thinking about them. I know it can't be easy for them either. Hopefully they get settled and in a school they like, make friends and get along. Betsy mentioned Jo talked about potentially moving close to us, so she'd be near some family, but I presume its just talk. It would be kind of neat though. I know my kids talk about them often and that would give them a chance to develop a better connection. Can't see it happening though.

Ross

Sent: Sunday, January 02, 2011 7:31 PM
Subject: Re: picture

Betsy,

I'm glad you guys liked the picture. I have a few that I really liked from that visit. If you could, send me some pictures, there weren't any left in the home of you all when I moved back in and I would like to have some. Enjoy the salmon, I have made that dip a couple of times during my trip to MI and it has been a big hit. Hope New Years was good, talk to you later.

Love, Steven

Date: Wed, Jan 5, 2011 at 9:39 PM

Subject: Re: picture

Steven,

Let's be honest with one another. We don't know each other. From the beginning, I haven't had a purpose in your life. "Hey Betsy, can I talk to Ross." For years, that was difficult for me. Because I think I am interesting. But I have gotten over this and for the last few years, it hasn't mattered. This Christmas you made a point to talk to me on the phone. Obviously, my past issues about you have been brought to your attention. Bravo for the attempt!

Let me get to present day so that I can present the issue that I am getting at. Ross doesn't lie or withhold information from me. He and I are extremely tight. Saying, "don't tell Betsy" isn't cool in my book. My marriage is very valuable and we love each other deeply. He is a wonderful man, a loving father and the best husband I could ask for. I'm sorry that you didn't have that in your marriage. But if you don't want your wife to find out about your girlfriend, then keep her a secret from EVERYONE until the divorce is final AND your children are able to process the fact that you are with someone other than their mother! Speaking as someone who has worked with children for the past 18 years, most of them are fucked up because of their parents. Children are self-centered, they feel responsible for and saddened by the faults of their parents. They will even feel like they caused whatever problems exist. Good luck in trying

192

to explain to them that you didn't choose this new woman over them. Good news though, children are forgiving, loving and very resilient.

Let me know when you are ready for a REAL conversation with me,

your sister-in-law,

Betsy

. . . . .

This email came a full year after Steven had given Jo the completed paperwork asking for a divorce and Jo had, in turn, falsely accused Steven of domestic violence; Steven never returned to the home again without a third-party present and never again initiated verbal contact with Jo. The children later expressed to us that "this was when their parents divorced."

. . . . .

There was not one question for Steven nor any show of concern for his wellbeing. Jo was very jealous and didn't like for Steven to have relationships with any women, including his familial relationship with Betsy. When Jo was not around anymore, Steven finally felt that he could reach out; he needed his whole family's support being so isolated and having lost his boys.

42 WHEN I WAS IN JAIL...

MY DUI COURT DATE GOT bumped up. I had hoped that I would be divorced by the time my DUI came out, but I appeared in court in April 2011. It was aggravated DUI because of my BAC, because the taxi had been hit and because I had run. I was sentenced to three weekends in jail. The Judge counted the weekend of my arrest, so I had two more to serve. I lost my license for forty-five days and had to attend court-ordered alcohol counseling.

My attorney counseled me to prepare for this day, to be ready to give over my license. I bought a bike with a carrier that attached to the back, so that I could transport my son. I also bought enough groceries to last the whole time. I had to maintain my schedule of DBT, individual therapy, alcohol counseling, full-time work, drop-offs with my son and all of his activities on a bike—all in rain or sunshine. My attorney told me to not even think about getting into my car on a suspended license, no matter how harmless it seemed. Things would get much worse if I was caught driving. I had messed up enough; I was not interested in getting into any more trouble, so I did not drive even once.

. . . . .

In order to serve my first weekend, I, once again, had to call my brother and sister-in-law for help. I didn't know what else to do. My sister-in-law drove me to jail, and handled my email and phone as though she were me, to help keep all of this secret from Peter. This was right before my son's Spring Break, so the plan was for her to pick him up right before she picked me up from jail, then I would have him with me for the week. She was going to stay with us the whole week, and take me to all of my appointments and to work.

I shared all of this with my rehab group and they gave me advice about how to make jail time as comfortable as possible. Wear layers, especially warm socks, it's cold. Stuff dollar bills in your socks and don't let anyone know that you have money. If I needed anything, I could negotiate using pop and chips from the vending machine. I was on my period, so I also stuffed tampons in my socks. This was the same advice that they had given to Sandy, months before.

. . . . .

I was again booked and strip-searched, and my tampons were confiscated. I had to request pads from the guard when I got in. I was
taken to a cell with glass walls, where there were ten other women.
Some watched a small television and others read. I got a book, got
on my bunk and started reading. The cells were on the first and
second floors, and there was an oval-shaped open area, also on the
first floor. There was a railing around the second floor (I was in a
cell on the second floor) and we gathered around the railing whenever there was a guard change. Every guard had their own individual
instructions in addition to the regular jail house rules. All of the non-
weekenders had jobs and some even left for off-campus jobs. During my stay, one of my bunkmates was taken to isolation—she
planned this so that she could just sleep all day and not have to
work.

When meals were served, we went down to get trays from the
food line and back to the cell to eat. After breakfast, there were
chores; after dinner, there was free time when we were all allowed
out into the common area. A couple of women were walking a circle
around the room as though it was a track, some were doing yoga,
some were talking, and others were in a small outside area. I was
called a "weekender" and there were eight of us, all in different cells.
One of the inmates was a yoga instructor and I tried yoga for the
first time, in front of a group of women who were watching and
commenting (Peter had not allowed me to do yoga because of its
association with non-Christian religions, which he felt opened up a
person to evil). I then walked the track with the yoga instructor and

196

while we did she told her story to me. She was busted for growing marijuana and they threw the book at her. She figured out how to live fairly well in jail and she would likely serve a year. Everything was unfair and nothing was her fault—the common theme in jail. Most of the inmates were mothers and were there for multiple DUIs or drug-related offenses. I didn't say much about myself or, really, much at all; I just read and listened.

. . . . .

One woman, who was truly trying to turn her life around and not just work the system, had a very unfortunate story. She had a newborn baby. The baby's father invited her over for dinner. He had been seeing someone else and she was heartbroken. She thought, with this invitation, he might want her back, so the dinner was very important to her. She arrived with their baby daughter, they ate and he served wine. When she left, he called the police and told them that she was driving drunk with their daughter in the car. She, not knowing what to do, called her mother and her mother told her to not let them breathalyze her. She might have been under the legal limit, maybe not, but because she refused the breathalyzer, the Judge ruled as if she had been at the aggravated level. Because she had her baby with her, she was serving four months. She found out that the whole evening was a set-up so that the baby's father and his new woman could be together and have the baby to themselves. She wasn't very emotional, just matter-of-fact. Her father was an alcoholic and taking a rehab drug called Antabuse, which was working for him. She planned to take it voluntarily, so that she never drank again. We talked about Antabuse.

. . . . .

"Antabuse blocks an enzyme that is involved in metabolizing alcohol intake. Antabuse produces very unpleasant side effects when combined with alcohol in the body....common products contain small amounts of alcohol, enough to cause an Antabuse reaction. Such products include aftershave, cologne, perfume, antiperspirant, mouthwash, antiseptic astringent, skin products, hair dyes and others [13]." Peter, the GAL and his attorney had decided that I needed to take this drug as part of my alcohol abuse consequence, in order to see my son. Me being a red head, I respond with superhero strength to medications. There are several studies that show those of us with red hair have a specific gene mutation, which makes us especially sensitive to pain and we have unique responses to anesthesia [14]. This medication was no different, and alcohol is in a surprising number of products. One day, I used lotion after shaving my legs and I had such a severe allergic reaction that I thought I might have to call 911. The GAL, Peter's attorney and Peter did not relent in their insistence upon this medication; I took it on and off. I was scared to take it, not knowing when I would have a reaction by eating something or using a product.

. . . . .

She still wanted to take Antabuse, even after hearing about my reactions to it.

. . . . .

The lights came on at "lights out" so that the guards could see into our glass cells, fluorescent lights, all night long. The next morning, we met around the railing for our morning instructions. We had to shower every day, eating was optional, but meals were served only at certain times and if we missed them, too bad. Common area time could be taken from us at any time, individually or as a group, depending on our behavior.

I did buy a pop for who appeared to me to be the alpha in the common area and I bought more for a few other women, just to be nice. The one good aspect of jail was that I had no responsibilities; I only had to care for myself and pass the time. The chores were nothing strenuous. I had not experienced this kind of freedom from responsibility for as long as I could remember.

Sunday morning, I was taken to the waiting area. I was glad to get out, and I was so excited to see my son and sister-in-law.

43 LISA PICKS ME UP FROM JAIL

I WALKED TO THE VAN where Lisa was parked and I got in. She looked worried. My son was not with her. She said, "This is bad, okay?" Peter found out. Those minutes in the van were so difficult; I was numb. My report and mug shots had been emailed and faxed to my individual therapist, to DBT therapist and to who-knows who else. There was an emergency hearing during which my time share was indefinitely suspended. I had earned a week with my son, unsupervised, because I was doing so well, adhering to everything that the court ordered. Suddenly, that was gone, I had nothing.

Both therapists said that the information came from the GAL, and that she had gone over the top. She sent several copies of my information, using different mediums. They both thought and said to me later something like, "okay we got it, Sabrina messed up—big time." Peter's attorney had set up some sort of alert and had picked up my booking.

I had done this to myself and to my son; I gave to everyone who was against me all the ammunition they needed, and they were more-than-willing to highlight this terrible night of poor choices and bad behavior. My boy was sad and he missed me; we had been so looking forward to a week together. I was devastated by what I had done. Lisa, however, did not judge me. She, instead, showered me with unending, unabashed love.

44 PEEING IN A CUP

WHEN LISA GOT HOME, SHE shared with my parents, who live close to her, the gravity of my situation. She and my brother lied to my parents, telling them that my license was taken away because I'd gotten into a car accident when I didn't have insurance. I had asked my brother and Lisa to tell this lie; they felt uncomfortable with it, but I just couldn't disappoint anyone else. Just as Peter had "saved me from my childhood," my parents were saving me from Peter. My story had come full circle. I couldn't disappoint them.

· · · · ·

My dad came to help me. He had a lot of questions and, sometimes, I felt that he was interrogating me. He was trying to comprehend why the Waltons weren't being reasonable. He couldn't believe it—

certainly, if I was nicer and negotiated, they would relent. By continuing to ask questions, he began to "get it." Like everyone else who was involved and supportive of me, he was appalled. He drove me around; it was really nice to have his help. He was outside of the courtroom when I was ordered to random alcohol urine testing. I had to call in everyday and, at least two times per week, I had to pee in a cup to be tested for alcohol. My first test was ordered for that day before 6:00 p.m. We made it just in time; my dad was such a good sport, hurrying to get me there.

I walked in, registered and waited to be called. There were trays of pee cups—pee was everywhere. I said to the registration woman, "Wow, has anyone told you it really smells like piss in here?" She smirked then took me back to the bathroom. There were mirrors in every direction and she stood at the door. She explained that I needed to pee in the cup and then give it to her. I said, "Well, hey, I feel like I'm in a porn with all of these mirrors and all." She laughed.

Every day I called in and I rearranged my schedule according to my pee-in-a-cup schedule. I travel some for work and I worried that when I was several hours away I wouldn't be able to get back in time. Once, I was four hours away and I was supposed to pee in a cup that day. I missed the cut-off time. I panicked and called my attorney. She assured me that everything would be ok; I had to work and it wasn't my fault. I had made it every other time.

. . . . .

One day I walked in and who did I see? Sally the stripper. I had some questions for her. A friend of hers had called me several times after the night of the DUI, trying to explain that Sally had tried to get me out of jail and had ended up getting arrested, herself. She said that Sally would pay back the money that they had borrowed. I was scared, thinking about what I had gotten myself into and what these people might do.

Sally was nervous to talk to me. She explained that she had tried to get me out of jail, but that the courthouse was closed. Her car had broken down and she had called my friend. She said that I should not trust my male friend, the designated driver the night of the DUI, that he was not really my friend. I'm not sure what she meant, but maybe it had something to do with women's clothes that were strewn all over my house, the day after the incident. They were probably Sally's, but what had she worn home? She didn't offer the whole story, and I didn't ask. It had been almost four months since the event and she claimed that she had been in jail in North Carolina for an alcohol-related offense and because of that, she was ordered to get randomly tested.

45 MY THIRD WEEKEND IN JAIL

SUSAN DROPPED ME OFF FOR my last weekend in jail. Susan and David are very conservative, so it was a big deal for them to not only support me, but also help me with jail time. They helped to transport me and my son, as much as they could, during the forty-five days without my license.

It was the same protocol. They booked me, took my mug shot, strip-searched me and then took me to my cell. I did yoga, read and listened, at times scared of the guards and of other inmates. The only difference was that this third time, sometime during the night before I was supposed to leave, they woke us up and moved several of us. The women in the cell to which they moved me were known as "trouble makers;" the guards shook things up to prevent inmates from getting too comfortable and from "making plans." I laid in my bunk with my eyes wide open. There was no way I would let myself sleep until I got home.

46 WEEKS BEFORE THE TRIAL

BECAUSE OF GOOD BEHAVIOR, I worked back up to visitation with my son. At first, time share was just a few hours, supervised by Susan. Then I was awarded workday overnights, then weekends.

. . . . .

Steven came for a visit several weeks before the trial. I had my son and I didn't know how to handle his visit. Peter was so hostile about exposing our son to my paramour—this was the worst thing I could possibly do. In retrospect, it was not a big deal; I should've been confident about Steven and not tried to hide him. In a "no fault" state, as ours was, infidelities don't matter.

I thought that if I had other people over along with Steven, then Peter could not identify Steven. Peter interrogated my son about me, so I didn't want to tell my son what to say or not say—he was already so in the middle. My future was with Steven. I was so eager to be done with the divorce that I offered a great deal to Peter, a better deal than he got in the end. Maybe I was being selfish to see Steven at this time, I don't know. We were in love and he helped me so much. Those at my gathering drank wine and beer; Steven had wine the whole time that he was there. I was on Antabuse and peeing in a cup; my son and I had juice.

Peter knew that Steven was there, so he sent my oldest daughter to knock on the door. I opened it and she demanded all of her childhood memorabilia. I was taken so off guard that I didn't know what to say. I certainly didn't want her to come in while Steven was there. I would've gotten her things together, but it would have taken too much time to get them all together. I told her this and she stormed off.

. . . . .

My younger daughter attempted suicide in the weeks before the trial. Peter did not contact me about this, insisting that I had borderline personality disorder and, thus, would make a spectacle. He said that I would be overly emotional and I'd make it all about me. I learned of the incident from my attorney only after my daughter was released from the hospital, where she had her stomach pumped. Peter blamed me for her suicide attempt and for her having THC in her system, saying that her ballerina friends had introduced her to drugs and that I had forced her into ballet, against her will.

Selfish or not, I am so thankful that Steven was with me when all of this happened with my daughters. This is one of the many truly heartbreaking moments in my journey.

47 DAYS BEFORE THE TRIAL

DAYS BEFORE THE TRIAL, MY attorney called me and asked me to come to her office. She emailed Peter's latest motion to me; it was bad. 1) I threw a party at which there was drinking. 2) Steven visited and I exposed my son to my paramour. 3) Steven showed my son how to start a fire. There were also some allegations about not treating my son's allergies. Peter's brother went through my garbage can, collecting empty wine bottles, empty beer cans, receipts that showed that I bought the alcohol and Steven's luggage tags. I bought wine for Steven and beer for my research assistant, who had worked overtime to meet a deliverable deadline for a grant—only one beer can had even been opened. I just couldn't stop doing stupid things. I had no defense against Steven's presence in my home. The worse allegation, the one that could've sent me back to jail, was that one of my pee tests had come back "diluted." I didn't know what that meant and neither did my attorney. Peter's team was using this as the proof that I had partied.

. . . . .

Again, Lisa was with me; my family was coming into town in a few days to support me during the trial. After I read the motion, Lisa held my hand while I curled up into a fetal position on the floor. I couldn't take much more.

Lisa drove us to the testing site; Steven was on the phone with me the whole time. I asked for my file and I asked them to explain what a "diluted test" meant. They said that my attorney had just been there, asking the same questions. The desk officer, with whom I had joked for months and in front of whom I had peed, was visibly upset for me. The site director was also there and he, too, had occasionally engaged in conversation and banter with me. He seemed affected as well. She explained that sometimes people who have had alcohol dilute their specimen by drinking so much water that results are inconclusive. Diluted results are failing test results.

48 ALMOST TRIAL TIME

August 2011

THE FOLLOWING EMAIL FINALLY GOT some people's attention, only after I underlined and highlighted all uses of the word "you." I was concerned about my son's constipation, worried that it was the result of the stress of the divorce and of being inappropriately touched by his Walton cousin. Peter was finally reproached for attempting to prevent our son from getting medical care. It was a turning point; the spotlight moved onto Peter.

Ms. Walton,

As agreed in our last parent coordination session, I am to be informed of the basic information pertinent to W's encopresis. This was reiterated in an e-mail from Ms. PC, received July 12th: "Information regarding W's chart continued to be shared between parents." You did not provide such information following your time with W July 21 thru 23. This is by no means exceptional. My attempt to simply assure that W has daily received the attention he needs remains unnecessarily difficult. On Sunday July 24th, the first full day following W's return to my care, he had three bowel movements.

Clearly W's toilet routine has improved dramatically since I initiated the medical intervention with Dr. P on March 21st. At that time you were highly resistant to W being seen by Dr. P, fearful, as you said in parent coordination, that I was simply using the situation to try to prove that his cousin was not the sexual predator you accuse him of being (your belief, confirmed in Dr. F's June 14, 2011 evaluation, was that the cousin was to blame for W's difficulties with encopresis). I tried to assure you that my intention was solely W's wellbeing. You relented only when I suggested that you were free to take W to his March 21st appointment. You took W to the follow up appointment with Dr. P on March 28th. Dr. P's note from that session indicates you reported W had been molested by a cousin. Obviously, at that time W's wellbeing was not at the forefront of your thinking.

The timing of your concern for W's medical needs is suspect. The end of the six-month regimen prescribed by Dr. P falls toward the end of September, 2011. Why, when you were hesitant to begin this process with W in the first place and have not taken the reporting seriously, would you initiate contact with Dr. P days before the final hearing in a year-long legal conflict? This is calculated chaos, and I would ask that you agree to maintain W's established routine and postpone this request. Dr. P didn't request an appointment with W until the end of the six-month period. Let's not combine another intensive clean out period for W with the emotional strain inherent in the final days of intensive legal proceedings.

My ongoing concern is that W's needs are not being placed at the forefront.

Sincerely,

Peter Walton

49 THE TRIAL

MY BROTHER AND SISTER-IN-LAW were at the trial, along with my dad (my mother was watching all of the children), Susan, Coco and my therapist. Peter brought our oldest daughter and Ben with him. The trial, itself, started at 10:00 a.m. Peter took the stand first and my attorney interrogated him for eight hours. Everything came out for the first time. Peter admitted to phone sex, going to massage parlors using a work vehicle from the children's home and the affair with Charlene while I was pregnant. My attorney shared the photos of my beaten face, the journals, my abuse, his control, everything.

· · · · ·

In the GAL's report/testimony she stated that Peter, after following up with the pediatrician, had indeed interfered with my son's medical treatment and that he needed to be seen immediately. If he had been under Peter's supervision, according to his email, my son would not have been treated, his condition would have been disregarded and dismissed.

The GAL interviewed my son about Peter's last motion, including the party and Steven. The GAL came to my home, this time to interview my son and when asked if I was drinking at the party, he said, "no, we were drinking juice," and he mentioned that his dad drinks. That opened up more questions and it came out that he, Ben and Mary Ellen had been drinking regularly. After that first hostile motion, the Judge ordered that neither of us drink. Ben, in his testimony, admitted to drinking about six times in my son's presence. The Judge admonished Peter, saying that he had been extremely concerned about my DUI, while continuing to drink, himself. He also asked Peter, rhetorically, "do you know how many people get a DUI during a hostile divorce... A lot."

. . . . .

My oldest daughter also took the stand against me and it was very damaging. My attorney did not cross examine her stating, "we don't believe the children, no matter what their age, should be involved in a divorce case, especially to testify against a parent." Then she sat down. My daughter looked surprised by this; she must have thought that we would go after her testimony. We never considered asking her a question, no matter how misrepresented I was.

. . . . .

Robin was incredible. She put me on the stand in the evening and Peter's attorney had only one point to make that had not been made already. That I had selfishly had breast augmentation. For me, it was a good decision. I was so insecure and ashamed of my body that I could not look at myself. Following the surgery, I felt good about myself. It was a much-needed boost to my self-esteem. I could start over, and part of this was that my sensuality and sexuality as a woman were fresh, new and voluptuous. I wasn't going to apologize for them and the Judge didn't comment.

Peter's attorney tried to push my buttons about my "paramour," so the Judge asked if anyone had any problems with Steven and asked if he had been interviewed. No one had, so no one could comment. I had made so many mistakes while trying to hide him. If only I hadn't been influenced by Peter, I could've saved myself and others so much grief in the days before the trial.

My attorney went through the timeline of financial abuse. When this got to the time that Peter quit the private school, just when we were finally getting on track and stable, the Judge said I was obviously angry and that he was not pleased with this display of emotion.

. . . . .

We stayed until after 11:00 p.m., the Judge saying he was going to finish the trial that day for my sake, that I had been through enough.

My therapist testified that the abuse that I experienced as a child was exaggerated by Peter and that I was suffering from PTSD mostly due to Peter's abuse. Years later, Peter mocked this testimony and called into question her credibility. She held a degree that Peter had attempted but failed to earn, and she was a woman.

Peter's attorney called the director of the testing center to testify about my diluted pee. He remembered me, and said that I was not a typical client. I was always positive and cooperative. When asked if he thought I had intentionally diluted the specimen he said, "no, if there was a problem, it is likely a medical issue." He had seen a lot of people come and go and, in his opinion, I was not working the system. I was running a lot, training for a half marathon. Running became my escape. I ran with my fists punching, visualizing winning the trial. Several times, my attorney passed me in her vehicle while I was out running, so she knew firsthand that this part was true. The dilution was more likely due to the amount of water I drank in order to make up for running in the July summer heat, than it was to an attempt to work the system. This contradicted what Peter's attorney had hoped to "prove." Though I was no longer required to pee in a cup after the trial, I went back to the testing center, just to thank the director.

The Judge ruled that I continue to pay child support, but much less than I had been; he stated that I was exhausted from working so much and that my retirement was mine, alone, so Peter received no percentage of it. I had taken forty-five-thousand dollars out of my retirement in order to pay for court and therapy expenses, so there wasn't much left, anyway. I kept the house and because the market was so upside-down, the Judge recommended that I rent out rooms to offset the mortgage until I could sell the house. He recognized that I would struggle to keep the house, with all of the debt and bills. He attributed each of our accumulated school debt to us, individually, and put all of the credit card debt on Peter; during the year, Peter tried to get me to file for bankruptcy, but I refused. He ruled that Peter keep a used Buick Regal and that we share joint custody. He used the schedule that I suggested, as I was the only one willing to negotiate time share.

. . . . .

Most importantly, for the first time my abuse was formally validated, the Judge ruled that I was a victim of domestic violence at Peter's hand and that I acted like a typical victim, by not turning him in and by back-peddling. He ruled that I had PTSD because of Peter and that our case would, from that moment forward, have a running head of "domestic violence case."

. . . . .

My attorney passed a note to me that said, "we won." Peter's attorney left the room hurriedly and without him; Peter left exuding anger and not looking at anyone. His attorney later filed paperwork saying he was not responsible for any negative outcome that came from this case because his client lied to him and, thus, he was not aware of information pertinent to the case.

Later, I learned of all the drama that took place in the hall outside of the courtroom that day. My oldest daughter screamed at her papa, my father, that he needed to stay out of it and he was not her papa. Susan had gotten to know my brother and sister-in-law; they developed a real connection and shared experiences supporting me; Coco was there and testified on my behalf, as a friend; my therapist waited all evening to testify. It brought me such joy that all of the people that I loved and who supported me came together just outside the courtroom door, standing by, ready to do anything to help me if they were called upon.

It was over. Could it be that it was—finally—really over?

50 THE FAMILY THAT STOLE CHRISTMAS

December 2011

MY SON AND I SHOPPED for weeks. We found the perfect gifts for his sisters. He often said, "maybe they'll love you again if you buy them nice things." We did buy them nice things. We talked about what they liked and about their favorite colors. I sold my engagement/wedding ring to a jeweler in exchange for jewelry for them—sentimental items, unique to their personalities. I spent the time away from my daughters, thinking and buying in anticipation of Christmas—our favorite family holiday. I thought that this was a way for me to connect with them and remind them of our relationship. Steven sat with me while I chose pictures from photo albums to put into their cards and selected special ornaments from their childhood. Every year, I had bought a *Hallmark* Christmas ornament for them, which they unwrapped Christmas Eve, and hung on the tree for the next day. I filled their gift boxes with these ornaments before I wrapped them.

Steven had visitation with his two boys and he had them with him this Christmas. His boys are one year and four years older than my son and the three got along very well, even better than we had expected. All blonde haired and blue eyed; they could be brothers. The boys played while Steven and I prepared for my son's exchange to Peter in the McDonald's parking lot Christmas Eve. We were court-ordered to exchange in a public location because of the domestic violence. We were going to drop him off, then head directly to his family. We wanted to get back so that it wasn't too late for his boys to enjoy the evening and the next day. I could've spent time with my son for part of Christmas day, but we didn't want to split Steven's time with his sons; he had not seen them since the summer.

The night before Christmas Eve, my son became unmanageable and emotional. After an hour of trying to calm him down, he revealed that Peter told him that I loved Steven and Steven's sons more than him. I asked my son why he would think that and he said, bordering on hysterical, "dad said the Judge let you have me on Christmas day and you said you didn't want me." I revealed my plans in court and, Peter relayed the proceedings to my son with the additional comment that I had chosen Steven's boys over him. I reassured my little man of my love and of his place in my heart. He was fine by the time we parted.

We all jumped in the car and drove to the exchange. I noticed that John Walton was sitting in the passenger seat and I was somewhat relieved to have a "neutral" person to help with the bags of presents. My son was concerned that he would not be able to carry them to his dad's car all by himself. I got out of the car and retrieved the bags of gifts that the boys were holding in the back seat, then walked across the parking lot. I stopped on the passenger side of the car and held out the bags looking for John Walton to help with the exchange of gifts, prepared to be polite. He looked straight ahead with a stern look on this face; he did not even glance in my direction. This highly religious man, leader in the church, had known me for twenty-four years and could not even acknowledge my presence. Peter stepped out to help my son and yelled for me to get away from his car, to not take one step closer. My son was crying. I panicked, threw the gifts in the car and said goodbye to him, whispering that it would be okay.

They drove around to the back and we followed. Peter stopped the car at a dumpster and proceeded to throw the gifts away. I opened my car door and started to film what he was doing, with my phone, so he put the gifts in the trunk of the car. I texted my daughters, "I just gave your dad hundreds of dollars' worth of presents. I think he was going to throw them out. I wanted you to know, please let me know if you get them." Twenty-one minutes later, I received a text from my oldest daughter, "thanks anyway. Just returned them in front of the P Clubhouse." Thirteen minutes after that, I received another from my youngest daughter, "Thanks anyway, they're at the clubhouse." I quietly sobbed, tears running down my face, for the entire six-hour trip to Steven's family. Steven asked me what he could do and I said to just please hold my hand. He did.

Steven said it was heartbreaking to watch me excitedly wrap the gifts, talk about my daughters opening them, write in the cards, select pictures… he knew that they would not accept the gifts; he had observed, second hand, their hostility toward me.

. . . . .

When we arrived at his father and stepmother's house, Steven took a call from his ex-wife. She had called dozens of times. He hadn't wanted to answer right in front of me while I was so distraught. She had left messages, obviously drunk, slurring her words, cursing and scolding. She yelled at him for about thirty minutes; this was one of the last times that he took a call from her, though she continued to harass him by phone for years. Instead of expressing concern over Steven and over what had happened with me, Steven's stepmother was upset at us for not having the boys talk to their mother.

Christmas Day, his stepmother made it very apparent that I was not welcome, though I had been vulnerable and had told her what happened with my daughters. I used the remaining money from selling my rings to also buy nice pieces of jewelry for Steven's stepmother and mother; I thought long and hard about the gifts that I bought for his dad, step-sister and the boys, all to show how much I cared about them and how much I appreciated them for sharing their holiday with me (and my son). Steven and I were having difficulties with the long distance part of our relationship and the stress of our ex-spouses was taking a toll on both of us. This can explain part of his stepmother's tone toward me. Also, one thing had changed since the previous visits when Steven's dad and stepmother were getting to know me: Betsy. She was now representing me to the family, without my knowledge.

Betsy become a portal for Jo; Jo used Betsy's willingness to engage in drama, to destroy me. I will explain this further in book two: Peter and Jo had begun to communicate. When Jo and Betsy talked, Jo relayed information that could only have come from Peter or from one of my daughters—the most humiliating information from my sealed divorce case, claims that I had painstakingly repudiated. She relayed false allegations and they had become the truth to Steven's family. No one talked directly to me, no one asked me anything, no one asked Steven anything, they shifted the way that they interacted, so that the stories about me circulated and amplified. All that I had experienced with the Watons was coming at me again, in nearly the same way, except with more intensity. Peter was able to continue to abuse me, re-victimize me again, with Jo and Betsy's help.

A year later, I still had to look at pictures of Steven's ex-wife all over his father and stepmother's house. Steven's stepmother constantly asked what his ex would want and she seemed scared to cross her in any way. Steven was an elite on SEAL Team VI, where he protected, defended, rescued and acted as guardian to our country, yet his own family didn't see him as a capable parent; they disrespected his choices. In contrast, Jo, an easily-agitated and sometimes violent woman, was seen as the legitimate parent and the family held her opinion in the highest regard. When I relayed all of this to my therapist, she said that when a forty year old brings a girlfriend home to meet his children and family, for the second Christmas holiday, the family should assume that the relationship is very serious.

My son and I came the day after Steven arrived, so that we could meet his sons, and we stayed a few days at his dad and stepmother's house before returning for the Christmas Eve drop off. I offered to give more time for Steven with his family and sons before our arrival, but he insisted that I come right away. This time, my son had to look at all of those pictures and he was confused. The boys seemed to have an immediate connection; they had a great time playing pool and having sleepovers in the living room. Jo Facetimed (FT) with her children too often for them to freely enjoy time with their father. When she did this, she asked to FT with my son, too. In a motion in Steven's case, she stated that not only were her boys not cared for, but that she also had to take care of my son over FT and that she helped him to get the medication that he needed—he was being neglected.

One morning, I was in the kitchen getting some medicine for my son, who was sick. Steven's stepmother looked at me with panic in her eyes and asked if it was for Thomas (Steven's older son); it was similar medicine to one he had taken. I said, "no," and she responded, "thank goodness." I felt a huge knot in my stomach and a lump in my throat. I was not welcome, the health and wellbeing of my son was of no concern. The evening before this, Steven's step-sister relayed stories of all of Steven's serious girlfriends, telling me specifically about an engagement and that this woman was the one who broke it off, implying that he had never gotten over her. His step-sister stated that this other woman was "the one" for him. She told me that his relationship with his ex-wife was very sexual and that their desire for one another was palpable—the only problem between them was that they approached parenting and life differently and their conflict was because of this.

. . . . .

I learned over time that the women in the family took it upon themselves to "understand and interpret" Steven and his relationships (without his input); they inserted themselves into the most personal parts of his life. Jo was more-than-happy to provide information about Steven to his family while he was deployed. Most often, this information was extremely negative; she was always the victim. I think they all had grown accustomed to this level of triangulation and didn't know how to handle Steven's involvement in a truly intimate relationship.

His step-sister believed that she understood Steven better than I did and she interpreted our relationship in the context of his other relationships. This behavior planted a seed of doubt and raised my insecurities. None of this information mattered enough to Steven for him to bring up with me; he had brought up other hurtful situations and relationships as part of his full disclosure to me. These women had a distorted view of Steven because they didn't take his own view into account. Steven consistently and without doubt countered their claims; I was the one, I was the only one, he waited his whole life to meet me and all others were just placeholders. He had never planned to have another serious relationship, so for him to jump all in with me was evidence of his feelings. I knew all of this, yet the doubt became louder in my mind leaving me sad, jealous, and insecure about Steven for years after. His stepmother wanted to have her step-son and grandchildren to herself. The whole family felt that Steven should spend time alone with his boys.

Steven was alone, isolated in Alaska without any family and with little support. His ex-wife was terrorizing him. He felt as hopeless, helpless and miserable as I did. We were each other's primary support and we deeply understood each other's anguish. Others' opinions about right and wrong didn't take into account how his wellbeing impacted his sons. Steven needed to be with me and I with him. Our being in a loving relationship was ultimately the best for the children. His children felt the family's disapproval toward me; this came out years later in their court-ordered therapy. This would drive a wedge in Steven's relationship with his father and stepmother, by putting him in an unnecessarily difficult and uncomfortable position.

. . . . .

I felt so uncomfortable that I wanted to leave. I was sick over leaving my son in so much suffering; I was missing him. I felt out of place and unwanted, but Steven wanted me to stay and he asked me to please not go. During the three years of our long-distance relationship, this was the only time I could not wait to leave Steven, to get away. I didn't know whether or not I wanted to continue a relationship with him because of how some of his family was acting— the opposite feeling from the one I had the previous Christmas. They broke us apart for a while. Six months later, my son was still talking about his horrific Christmas Eve with his therapist. That "vacation" layered more PTSD onto all of us.

51

WHY DON'T YOU KEEP SENDING THEM

CARDS AND PRESENTS?

WE WERE ALREADY DOWN THE road and could not take the time to go back and retrieve the presents. I called Susan, who was the only person I knew to be in town, and could barely explain what happened through my sobs. David and Susan gladly picked up the gifts; they have always been there for me.

. . . . .

Both my father and I have to talk to everyone: cashiers, bank tellers, people waiting in line, etc. We strike up conversations with anyone who will listen. While I was selecting gifts for my daughters, during my repeated trips to the mall, I, of course, discussed my girls, how excited I was about their presents and the ways in which they would likely use the apparel, purses and shoes.

When I returned home, I planned to take back the clothing and of-the-moment items, and to save the jewelry. I went over to David and Susan's house and unwrapped the gifts. Susan thought she should go with me to return them, because I was, again, extremely upset. We went to the store and the same sales clerk was there. She asked me how my girls liked the presents and I began to sob, a sob where unavoidable sounds come from your guts. We had to leave. A few weeks later, as tears ran down my face, I made it through the return. I cannot enter that store to this day.

. . . . .

My friend, J, whose then-twenty-six-year-old daughter hasn't spoken to her for years, for many of the same reasons that stand between my daughters and me, says that she stopped giving gifts when her daughter returned a birthday present to her front porch. J and I have an unfortunate bond of shared pain; I am so thankful for her vulnerability and for her willingness to be there with me, every step of the way. For some reason, the rejection of gifts is devastating for both of us.

. . . . .

People who mean well recommend that I still send cards and gifts, that I not let up on my girls. I cannot bear it again. It hurts way too much to be rejected by my own flesh and blood. Even as I write this my heart tightens and tears run down my face. I have to be able to function, to be a productive employee and a good parent to my son. Susan tells me, when I start to second guess myself, "they rejected you, not you them, and you were a good mom; you have to wait patiently for them to take a step toward you." She's right; though it hurts so much, it feels right. To do anything other than this leaves me vulnerable to an emotional crash. It feels like death; I mourn for them daily. And then I stop myself, every day, hope and pray that they are well and will someday be able to free themselves from the Waltons, to move just one inch toward me. Then I turn away from the pain and darkness and look at my new path with the sun shining brightly on it. I wish they would walk with me just once and a while.

52 SOCIAL SERVICES GETS INVOLVED AGAIN

DIVORCE DOES NOT BRING FREEDOM from a sociopath. It brings a degree of freedom, but it's not complete. In March 2012, I had been divorced for seven months and I had not spoken to Peter, without a witness, for more than two years. Peter filed a false report with social services saying that I was abusing my son, who was then eight. He planted a memory. Sociopaths are masterful at creating memories and distorting reality. It went nowhere, but something like this always brings doubt on the accused. This happened days before he announced that he was moving back to Canada, an unlikely coincidence. This prompted me to start a blog.

. . . . .

"Abusers often try to manipulate the "system" by:

- *Threatening to call Child Protective Services or the Department of Human Resources and making actual reports that his partner neglects or abuses the children.*

- *Changing lawyers and delaying court hearings to increase his partner's financial hardship.*

- *Telling everyone (friends, family, police, etc.) that she is "crazy" and making things up.*

- *Using the threat of prosecution to get her to return to him.*

- *Telling police she hit him, too.*

- *Giving false information about the criminal justice system to confuse his partner or prevent her from acting on her own behalf.*

- *Using children as leverage to get and control his victim* [15]."

. . . . .

Following the divorce trial, Peter used free services to continue to abuse and harass me. I was on a work trip in Orlando, Florida when I received the call alleging I was physically abusing my son. For my boy's sake, as well as my own, I needed this to stop. What did I need to do to stop being victimized? Could I do anything? Could I ever stop fearing Peter and the rest of the Waltons? My own thoughts and fears were giving Peter and the Waltons power over me. How could I overcome my fears and take back my power? I could do and think the exact opposite of what I had been conditioned to do and think.

I "friended" on Facebook anyone that I could think of that had been or was then both in the Waltons' social circle and in mine. I friended hundreds of people from John Walton's past congregations and Elaine's former co-workers, along with friends of Peter, Jack, Mary Ellen and Ben. I was going to use social networking to expose them. I was going to be the opposite of a victim. It was going to take a great deal of strength; I would be criticized, so I needed thicker skin. I was going to take back my power, stop being afraid and make my story public.

. . . . .

Perpetrators thrive on their victims' secrecy and embarrassment. By me telling my own story, with all of my most embarrassing and shameful moments, revealing my flawed self and my misbehaviors, I actually take back my story. They don't own it and they can't control who hears what parts anymore.

. . . . .

I posted the cover picture of this book as my profile picture on Facebook with a comment that I plan to spend the rest of my life fighting domestic violence, and I thinly veiled the fact it was Peter.

I was criticized and critiqued by some, but the support was un-fathomable. Friends reported that some of the Waltons were post-ing scripture versus hinting that they were the victims of my vicious attacks. If they would've simply left me alone and not tried to take everything from me, I never would've said anything; I would've just moved on and not looked back. Like most victims, I wanted to get as far away from Peter as I could, have as little communication as possible and get him out of my mind and soul. However, there was another path for me and it would be difficult and humiliating at times.

The next day I took down the photo; I was still scared. Later I posted it again and, this time, I left it. My fear and anxiety lessened. When Peter tried to hurt me, whether it be emails or false allega-tions, I posted the picture again. I also blogged about it. I don't think it occurred to any of the Waltons that I would say anything, much less do the unthinkable.

53 POST-DIVORCE COURT HEARINGS

BY AUGUST 2012, I'D HAD my son full-time for more than six months, though I had continued to pay child support to Peter. I learned that he was making a salary of least seventy thousand dollars and still gladly accepting my child support.

I finally filed a motion to terminate child support and to ask for, at least, day care help from Peter. I didn't want to ask for child support from him: I knew that it would ignite his anger and renew his threatening and intimidating behavior, drawing out my fear.

Three court dates later, he wanted a fourth—he represented himself. He saw the actions that I initiated in court against him as an opportunity to tattle tale on me. He thrived on the attention that court hearings brought—unaware that he was seen in a negative light. It was a simple math equation, but somehow he, again, made it into a circus. This is why it took me six months to take action; it was worth the money to have peace and lessen my anxiety over what he might do.

Re-engaging with Peter in this way left me on heightened alert. Between court dates one and two, I learned that Peter had my heat turned off. The gas company explained that though I was paying directly from my bank account, he was still on the account and, therefore, had the legal right to terminate service. I had paid for a service man to fix my heating only to learn it had been turned off. It took the gas company a week to turn it back on. During that time, the vent on the outside of the house had been broken and the gas company left a note, followed up by a formal letter, saying it was a safety hazard and to not turn on the heat. The man hired to fix my heat came back and said that the vent had not been like that the week before; he was surprised when I called. These events occurred the week before court appearance three. This left me paranoid and even more afraid. I was glad I had the housemates to whom I had rented rooms in order to cover court costs and the mortgage.

. . . . .

I have been asked quite often why I didn't leave Peter earlier if I thought he might kill me. In addition to the reasons that I've revealed in this book, the biggest factor is fear.

. . . . .

My attorney represented me on court date two, because I did not want to face Peter in court. For court date three, the Judge called him in Canada. I stood in front of the bench as our income was reviewed. Peter, in a condescending tone said, "do you think rental income should be reported Ms. Walton?" My attorney jumped in and said that I had reported that income to her, that she had forgotten to include it and that it was her fault; she quickly provided the information. He went on quickly "and what about your blog income… your Honor, this blog is ruining my family… I hope, Ms. Walton, that you are reporting all this to the IRS… she is posting court-related information in a closed case… you will be hearing from me about this blog… we will address that in court." I turned to the Judge and said, "yes, I have a blog." The Judge asked how much I had made and said that it did not need to be included. The Judge told Peter that he could ask any question of me about the renters. Peter proceeded to ask me if I understood that rent money was income and if I'd thought to bring that up to the Judge. Peter went on to ask, again, if I understood that taking money from people who are living with me is income and did I understand that it was devious to not report it [still no real question]. I said his questioning was didactic. After several more rounds, the Judge said to Peter that we were moving on. He tried one more time, and the Judge said, "are you still on the renters? We've resolved that and included the rent." He did the calculation and ordered Peter to pay child support to me. I nearly said to the Judge "no, thank you." There was no way that he would pay this to me, regularly, without some sort of retaliation. The Walton's were likely plotting. I was afraid of what he/they might do. I was filled with panic for the entire weekend.

The rapid-fire didactic questioning was devastating to me in any setting, especially in court. This distracting chaotic confusing tactic was so familiar to me. He waited, forfeiting the chance to prove his point with documentation; his stronger craving was to knock me off balance and possibly bring out a reaction/emotion from me. In court, I thought my legs might give out from under me, my body and voice trembled with every word. My thoughts were to 1) shut down the blog and 2) say no to the money. My feeling was fear. I was a professional woman who had supported myself since age seventeen; why in the world was I having this irrational reaction?

I have post-traumatic stress disorder from Peter, which means that current events can trigger feelings from an old event, so my feelings don't necessarily match the situation in the moment. My actions don't have to match my triggered thoughts and feelings, so I will continue to blog and take the money. In time, my thoughts and feelings will match current events without detouring through the time machine.

. . . . .

At fifteen, of course I had a personality, but I had yet to be an individual in the adult world. While I was developing into an adult emotionally, mentally and spiritually with the world a wide open field of opportunity, these four walls slammed down around me; my world became smaller and smaller. The voice I heard was Peter's while all other voices got quieter. My dreams faded, replaced by daily practical life—how to feed a baby and simply survive, all the while entangled with the Waltons. Life is hard enough with a partner who loves and gives; with a sociopath, the victim's individuality deteriorates. When Peter finally moved out, I didn't know my favorite color, what music I liked, what television programs or movies interested me, what clothes I liked, my overall style, who my friends were, why I wasn't talking to my family, what perfume I liked, what to do with free time, what food I liked, or who I was. I was thirty-nine years old and, for the first time in twenty years, I was in charge of my time and my being.

His voice, in 2012, was still loud and his manipulations were still effective, but by then I could turn my back, walk away and find other voices that were willing to build me up, walk with me and love me for me.

54 IT'S REALLY RED

A FRIEND AND COLLEAGUE, WHO was following my blog, mentioned a television show that reminded him of Peter. This show is a popular detective show and the suspect was being interrogated. To determine if he was lying, detectives set a plate of cookies on the table and left the room. They observed him eating a cookie through the two-way mirror. The detectives returned to the room and asked the man if he had eaten a cookie. He said no, so they explained that they had watched him eat the cookie and he denied it again and again.

· · · · ·

A year before Peter finally left, I found web addresses on my work computer that he wasn't even trying to hide. One was "How to

Catch a Cougar," and there were other dating websites. I confronted him and he denied it, without flinching, over and over again. I showed him the websites, went to them and showed him the time and date that he was on them (while I was at work, during the day). He did not waver.

. . . . .

During the year-long divorce proceedings, Peter took documents to my son's elementary school. I believe that they were motions, but, whatever they were, I was completely cut off from my son while he was at school, though I never lost joint custody. I was escorted off of the school grounds three times and not allowed to pick him up for therapy or medical appointments. I was told that they needed documentation that countered what had already been filed at the school. The parent coordinator at that time sent documents and called the school; the GAL and my attorney did, as well. Still, the school would not let me take my son out of the building and I was not allowed into the building for most of that year. Finally, the parent coordinator sent the final divorce decree which stated joint custody. Peter not only repeatedly denied ever taking anything to the school or talking to anyone, he was infuriated that everyone would make such accusations against him.

Peter was so angry that he threatened to make a formal complaint to the American Psychological Association against the parent

coordinator, who dared to cross him. She also had, in sessions, begun to challenge him. She quit, of course. I believe that this is the
reason that others involved feared to take a stand against Peter.

55 UNTIL DEATH DO US PART

WRITINGS FROM VICTIMS OF SOCIOPATHS all say the same thing: the perpetrators cannot and will not move on. They can re-marry, have other children, even move to another country and still, they remain fanatical about a relationship long gone. They behave and talk in a way that makes it appear that the relationship continues.

. . . . .

Long after Peter and I no longer talked to each other at all, he still talked about me to my son, daughters and our legal liaisons as though we were interacting in the same way that we had while we were married. He assumed and predicted my actions as if I were the same person I had been while I was living with him. He did this with such tenacity and persuasiveness that it took years for people, new to our story, to see through his manipulative ways. I dreaded anyone new being brought into our case.

I once asked my son, when he was eight, if his dad and his sisters ever said things about me that he knew weren't the truth. He smiled, wondering how I knew that, and said yes. I asked him if it was confusing. He said it was confusing all the time. He didn't understand and he expressed to everyone involved in our divorce case that he didn't understand why "everyone hates mom." He also shared that Peter would talk very negatively about Steven and one day he responded, "how do you know, you've never met him?"

. . . . .

In April 2012 I received an email from our new parent coordinators. Court-ordered parent coordinators were intended to keep us out of the court system. We had two because I asked to not ever be in a therapeutic situation with Peter; we each had one and they negotiated with each other, representing each of us. I could no longer put myself in a position where he could have any influence over me and, at that time, I was still scared of him. I needed communication with him to slow down so that I had time to process, alone, and not fall into old patterns.

I had to start over from the beginning with the new parent coordinators. By abruptly moving to Canada without changing time

246

share orders, Peter gave up his rights to fifty-fifty time share, unless he came back for his time. There is a completely different set of rules when custody becomes international. Even so, the parent co-ordinators stated that it was "risky" for me to prevent fifty-fifty time share. It was risky for me to let him go.

56 I WISH THAT MY STORY WAS OVER

BY JULY 2012, NOTHING HAD been worked out. Legally, I didn't need to do anything; I could simply sit back and wait out the summer. Peter needed to take the initiative and file for a new schedule, one that accommodated a parent moving out of the county, state and country. Because he moved without initiating this, his actions were considered child abandonment. With minimal communication attempts after ten weeks, I didn't need to allow him to see his son even during his scheduled weekend times. Twice, my son sat on Skype waiting for Peter to call him during their two scheduled sessions per week. He sat in his Canada shirt waiting for thirty minutes, both times. The same man that kept me in court for more than a year, claiming that I was an unfit mother, did not appear too bothered about his son, now. His fight for sole custody had more to do with my love for my son than his love for his son. He had lost many parental rights by this point. Keeping this in mind, I received an email, "I would like to put an agreement in front of you to sign before having the attorney submit the document to the Court," referring to a legal document from an attorney in Canada about visitation from then forward.

From Canada he was trying to dictate, control and take care of everything. Bringing in an attorney at all is a hostile and intimidating maneuver—completely unnecessary. The purpose of parent coordination is to keep families out of the courts and to keep money in the home for the children.

. . . . .

In the midst of this, a social worker showed up at my door. The allegations, from four months prior, were still unresolved. It was an unsettling reminder of Peter's tenacity.

. . . . .

Thinking about that summer break, I considered many things: my daughters and their brainwashing by the Waltons, their potential additional negative influence on my son's little brain; he might be kidnapped; Peter could claim that my son was reporting further abuse to stall his return; it was possible that I would have no contact with my son during his visit.

I was conflicted. My son wore his Canada shirt and he wanted to see his dad. If I didn't allow him to visit, would I be doing the same thing that Peter had done—using our son as a pawn? I called Peter; he had not changed. It was not good for me to talk with him. Though he did not illicit an outwardly emotional reaction from me, he did affect me and he used information about my daughters against me. It hurt; I never called again. We did, however, agree to a schedule. I reluctantly dropped my son off and allowed visitation in Canada for almost five weeks. During the visit, we Skyped. When my son wasn't alone, when we Skyped, he would not speak, but only type messages to me.

57

THE LITTLE MAN'S PERSPECTIVE

ON SUMMER BREAK

Summer 2012

IN JANUARY 2017, WHILE DRIVING my son home from school, he started asking about this book. I had talked a lot about it, trying to meet a specific launch date. He asked what it was about and when he could read it. I told him briefly about some of the content and said it was like an R-rated movie, so he wouldn't be able to read it until he was an adult. He asked if he was in it and I said, "yes about as much as Steven is," and he smiled. He then began to freely relay stories about Canada.

. . . . .

He said that he remembered sitting for hours on the living room rug at John and Elaine's house, playing while the Waltons, Peter and his sisters talked about me and our situation. He said that he chose to stay and listen and that they didn't know that he was comprehending what they said. He said they were always very mean about me and that they talked about me a lot. What most concerned him was that he had heard the word "kidnap." He couldn't remember if it was while he was with the larger Walton family or just when Peter and his sisters talk together, without anyone else around. He just remembers hearing the word several times. He also heard conversations in which all of the Waltons talked about, "what if he didn't go back, was that possible, what would that look like?"

My son then described, in detail, like it was yesterday, his daily routine when he was with Peter and not with the extended family. Peter left for work at 8:00 a.m. and took the subway; our son went with him. My boy thought that he would be able to escape during this time if anything out of the regular routine happened; he thought that he might be kidnapped. He said that the subway would be underground, then above ground and that there were spaces between the concrete where he could see life above the subway. He had memorized the route and the names of different stops. There was one stop where he had seen a pay phone. If he noticed anything different with Peter (more bags, a different route), he would escape off the subway and make it to that phone. He made sure to always have enough change in his pockets. Then, he would call me and tell me where his safe place was and wait for me until I could save him.

. . . . .

Peter and his family moved so much, and Peter continually changed his address, just a little, on documents, so that I never knew exactly where he was (so that and he could later say that he didn't receive court-related documents). My son stayed with other immediate family members and extended family members, and attended camps with cousins. I really didn't have a grasp of where he was at any given time. Peter had moved from Toronto to Ottawa and had not notified me; I learned of the move when my son relayed on Skype that he was in Ottawa. Because of this uncertainty, this lack of permanency and security, my son always had to be awake and aware when traveling with Peter. He memorized signs and asked questions as if he was curious about geography. He learned what states and provinces he was travelling through and he was always on guard, watching for variations from the route. I did not know this, but my intuition was spot on; kidnapping was a real threat, and, if the legal process that we went through in order to divorce was any indication, it could take years to get my son back.

. . . . .

Steven had colleagues that lived in Ottawa. He had alerted them to what was going on; he and they were standing by if my boy needed to be saved. When we told all of this to him, in 2017, he was surprised that we had considered what he had actually been going through and he seemed very happy to learn that Steven was protecting and watching over him, even back then.

58 IN PETER'S OWN WORDS

IN SEPTEMBER 2012, I POSTED to my blog:

"If you don't write with tears in your eyes….I can only think of them for a little while and then I have to change my thoughts before I start to feel very deep emotional loss. My daughters….they are gone. I remember carrying them for nine months. I can still feel them kicking and growing. A mother's body changes so much in pregnancy. It's the great equalizer having children—an experience where no woman goes untouched. Nine months of attaching to another human being. I have loved them and given them my twenties and thirties. They were always primary in my mind. I worked, provided and took risks I never would have without them. I gave up opportunities that are no longer an option for me—I gave them my youth. I chose to carry and keep my daughter as a teenager. I launched into immediate and intense responsibility, not able to lean on anyone else."

. . . . .

Both girls danced at the professional level; both were beautiful and breathtaking when they performed. My oldest daughter eventually moved on to opera—her natural talent; the younger could've danced for years as a professional—she was a natural. Peter characterized me as one of those crazy pageant show moms and our younger daughter quit ballet; I don't know whether or not my oldest is still performing opera. She threatened early on that if I attended one of her performances, she would have me arrested.

I had sacrificed quite a lot, and spent a lot, for my girls, trying to help them find and excel in their areas of talent and interest. I spent hours at ballet studios and voice lessons, most days of the week, doing my homework and my work at the studios. After my son was born, he spent hours with me at the girls' activities. My therapist pointed this out when she testified at our trial, "What had Peter been doing while you were working, going to school, transporting the girls, with your son with you most of the time? He was a stay-at-home dad—how was he helping?"

. . . . .

I know I chose this and chose Peter to have children with. I can't believe I did. My son does not understand why they will not talk to me; he says their reasons don't make sense to him.

By September 2012 I had finally taken all of their pictures down and would try not to think of or feel the intense void. When I respond to well intending people that my daughters don't speak to me—their last words to me delivered in screams and that the last time I tried to hug my middle child she dialed 911, leaving, her then seven year old, brother hysterical—they generally respond "they'll come around.."

I don't foresee having a relationship with my daughters for a very long time, if ever. Peter is so masterful at twisting and turning reality to such a degree, and with so many lies, that I can't anticipate, much less counter, what he says to them.

The parental alienation is likely intensifying in order to keep the façade going; as more time passes, the obvious question is "if she were a terrible mother, what is she doing now to promote such an extreme response?" There will be unending situations that were or are my fault, and new hypotheses about their estrangement from their mother. The best way to explain this phenomenon is to share, in Peter's own words, the irrationality with which I continued to live.

. . . . .

I've changed only the names in an email that I received in September 2012 regarding a week-long vacation of mine. I gave Peter the right of first refusal, which means that he had the first option to take his son. He declined, so I gave the itinerary of our son's care to Peter one month prior to the trip.

Sabrina,

You haven't left very much time for a response to your unilateral decision to leave W for a week. You communicated this to me by email in the middle of the night, probably as you prepared to fly out this morning - perhaps you are in the air now. This is not full disclosure. W benefits from knowing that both his parents know what is going on. He will be aware of the fact that I was in the dark on this plan. All that was communicated to me was that you would be gone over Labour Day weekend. I reported back that I would unfortunately be unable to leave Toronto due to two looming by-elections. What prevented you from being completely transparent about your plan? Will you put your own comfort aside for W's sake? Perhaps you agreed with my suggestion a few weeks back that it would be in W's best interest for you to not go on the trip at all.

Did you assume I wouldn't want to be part of planning for his week, had I known you were leaving? I do. I would like W to spend the weekend with his Uncle Ben Walton and Aunt Mary Ellen Walton. What prevented you from suggesting this from the beginning? Isn't this clearly in W's best interest? Please inform Susan and David that Ben would be delighted to pick up W at their place on Friday evening, say 6pm, and return him on Sunday at 6pm. W wants to have contact with his cousins. It doesn't make sense to deprive him of the

257

opportunity to interact with his family, especially considering they live a mere five-minute drive from you.

As you launch into another vacation, I hope you will pause to consider these matters for W's sake.

Thank-you, Peter

· · · · ·

I responded by re-sending the already-provided detailed itinerary. I had waited for Peter's response, made other arrangements and notified him. I also indicated that I would have limited cell phone coverage, making it even more imperative that everything was set before I left. Peter called my phone during my kayaking trip, more than he had in the entire time since our divorce.

· · · · ·

Sabrina,

Your statement: "I cannot wait until the last minute" is confusing. I'm suggesting you have indeed waited until the last minute to inform me on planning this week-long vacation, and it is not in W's best interest. I didn't even imply it was an obligation for you to have W interact with Ben and Mary Ellen, cousin and cousin. I was suggesting it is in W's best interest to do so. I am asking you to consider that blocking him from interacting with his family is not in his best interest. I am asking you to consider W, and not yourself, and your comfort level. He has clearly expressed to me a desire to interact with my brother and his

258

cousins. I'm not sure how yet another accusation, this one against my father, helps W in this case. Will you please stop targeting seemingly anyone associated with me and focus on W's well-being? Here, you freely target my father without considering what he means to W. Have you considered the energy my father has poured into building a relationship with W. W clearly loves my dad.

W loves his sisters as well, and they truly love and value him. It is entirely inappropriate for your personal and inexplicable vendettas to prevent W from freely developing relationships with both his sisters. They are beautiful young women of character. Don't you agree more not less needs to be done by you to promote these relationships along with W's relationships with my brother's family? Targeting your own daughters to attempt to mask your gross dereliction as a mother is becoming increasingly difficult, I'm sure. At some point you may need to face reality. I can understand your reticence to do so. I would ask again that you consider W's relationships to me, to his sisters, and to his extended family. W's dental visits and medical visits are certainly important. I appreciate you taking care of those responsibilities. What I am addressing here is a different matter, W's emotional well-being.

Regarding this weekend, it is not too late. All that you need to do is let the Susan and David know that my brother will pop by to pick up W for the weekend. Will you make that one call and get back to me to confirm. W would much rather spend the weekend with his family than with an older couple [Susan and David].

Thank-you, Peter

. . . . .

After a few more of these and the phone calls that I did not take, I implored the parent coordinators to have Peter stop badgering me during a much-needed and well-planned escape from the world of computers. He did not stop.

. . . . .

What becomes clearer to me as time passes, is the misery that Peter must live in, all the time, blaming anyone near him for the things that he doesn't like. There is an incredible and interesting life awaiting the victims of sociopaths, if they can just get away. The cast of characters with whom I spent the week were fun and free, things that I had never experienced. Even a group like this, even while on vacation, I could not stop talking about my daughters and about how I miss them, always with tears in my eyes.

59 STILL MAKING MISTAKES

IN OCTOBER 2012, MY SON was on the phone with Peter while he sat next to me. He kept putting the phone on speaker and playing with it. I hear Peter say, more than five times, to "tell your mother" this and that. I finally hit my threshold; I grabbed the phone and said to Peter, "If you have an adult matter that you need to discuss with me, you can email me and copy our parent coordinators. This is a child and should not be involved in adult matters. Say goodnight; our son needs to get to bed." I was rude and unprofessional; my son was crying. He said to me, "you were mean to my dad." I messed up. I looked him in the eye and said, "yes, I was and that is your dad and I was wrong. I'm sorry I made you feel uncomfortable." He stopped crying. What I said was okay, just not in front of our son. I needed to be very careful, to take the higher road, to be the parent to whom he feels comfortable expressing himself, to be the parent with whom he feels safe, the parent to whom he can at-

tach.

60 HAPPY BIRTHDAY TO ME

November 2, 2012

THE FOLLOWING EMAILS WERE WRITTEN after Peter had again been ordered to pay child support and after I revealed that I was taking my son to see Steven.

The string of emails ended with one from my attorney:

Peter,

At this point you have zero credibility with the court. This fact is readily apparent. You lost at trial on every single point. Plus no parent who has the concerns you alleged in the past or allege at this time would have moved away to another country and left their child here. So, I would suggest that you stop your threats and accept that you no longer control Sabrina's every move.

. . . . .

It started with an email that I wrote on Thursday, November 1, 2012:

Peter,

This is to inform you that W and I will be traveling to Norfolk, VA next week. Steven is having emergency surgery so we will leave right after my Wednesday class 11/7 and arrive at The Naval Amphibious Base, Little Creek by 2:00 a.m. 11/8. We will return home Saturday 11/10. I have already spoken to W's principal and teacher about W missing school and it is perfectly fine (I didn't have time to complete an educational enhancement request). He is allowed 10 absences for purposes like this.

Before being bombarded by criticisms, I would like to add that W will get to meet many men serving actively in Special Forces, see several bases and watch current operation training. The principal thought this to be an excellent opportunity for W. Additionally, Steven (and his boys) will be part of W's immediate family soon; he is important to us and it is important that we are there at this time.

. . . . .

Peter responded on November 2, 2012:

Sabrina,

Once again, you are dictating W's agenda without even a hint of dialogue with me. I do not in any way agree with you taking W out of the state and out of the established two-hour driving radius we agreed on nearly two years ago now.

The clear way forward here is for W to remain with Ben and Mary Ellen and attend school each day of your absence….I only have time to lay out bullets, but I will be happy to clarify anything that remains unclear here. W has missed nearly 20% of his school year thus far. Half of his absences are unexcused. You wrote that you don't have time to complete an educational enhancement request. Why not? If you did have conversations with W's principal and teacher I'm not at all certain I agree with your take away from the conversations. Both Ben and Mary Ellen are teachers. They interact with many teachers. A 20% absentee record is a concern. W needs to remain in school, not miss at least two more school days (It could be more days because you have a tendency to distort the actual length of your trips. Recall in August when you informed me Wednesday morning at 1am of your departure that morning. I was told you would be gone only for Labour Day weekend. Then you refused to consider Ben making a five minute trip to pick up W so he could spend time with them. You told me to stop "harassing" you while you were "vacationing".

I am not at all convinced W's education will be enhanced on a trip of this nature. When you had Skype sessions with W from Alaska this summer you were highly intoxicated. [My Skype sessions were at noon and 4:00 p.m. AK time and I was working]

It was clearly visible and it was obvious based on what you were saying and how you were saying it (I'm not confusing this with the static that exists over long distance Skype sessions). You do not need to involve W in your heavy drinking with Steven, who also has a drinking problem. You wrote that both you and W need to be with Steven during this time of his surgery. This is not true. You can't airbrush people in and out of a child's family. Steven is important to you at this time. W's relationship to Steven is not your relationship to Steven. W doesn't need to be present for whatever is going on in Virginia (You claim this is emergency surgery. The surgery is presumably a week away and 3,000 miles from Steven's current residence). If Steven is having a surgery, then go to Virginia and leave W to take care of W's business. W needs stability. Why do you not take advantage of the stability that Ben and Mary Ellen can offer you, and on a regular basis? They live five minutes from your residence.

When I exercised my prerogative in the spring, as part of the findings of the court, to have you establish the Skype breathalyser testing…. Do you remain unwilling to comply with the order?

W doesn't travel particularly well. What you are describing is a trip into the middle of the night on Thursday morning, after a long day Wednesday. Then you are suggesting coming back on Saturday. This is a difficult trip. What is your plan if W begins to vomit as a result of motion sickness at around 11pm on route to Virginia? He could alternatively be asleep in a comfortable bed in his own room at Ben and Mary Ellen's home, and be ready for school Thursday morning.

Despite your attempts to create a narrative of a well put together family of five—you, Steven, Steven's two sons and W—you are doing so despite the bald facts. Both you and Steven suffer from alcohol dependency….. W and I have an unbreakable bond that you seem intent on disrupting.

Maybe there is a better trajectory. Your relationship to Steven doesn't have to include the illusion of a neatly put together family life. A rocket scientist is not necessarily a good parent; it's not an intelligence thing. Parenting is ultimately about nurturing bonds, it's about relationship…I do have a degree of social intelligence. I know my children and can effectively help them navigate their

*way forward. A desire on your part to carve me out of W's life and transplant
a false narrative does not benefit W.*

*I don't know what is really going on here Sabrina, but consider W. Confirm
that W will go to Ben and Mary Ellen's for the entire time you are gone. He
doesn't need to be part of whatever is going on in Virginia. He won't tell you
that he would prefer the stability of remaining at home with a family that cares
deeply for him. He wants to please his mother and preserve a semblance of stability.*

Do you remember the driveway scene toward the end of Sherrybaby?

. . . . .

He meant for the last sentence to be the most hurtful and disparaging remark. *Sherrybaby* is a movie about a heroin addict that can't
take care of her daughter, and, in the end, acknowledges this and
asks for help. Peter implies with this statement that I need the help
of his brother in raising my son because Peter, himself, is not there.

. . . . .

Nothing I say or do affects Peter. School is an important monitoring
tool in custody cases and Peter continued to use this avenue to harass me for years to come. Thankfully, my son is well-above average
in math and he scores very well on standardized testing. I home
schooled my oldest daughter when she was his age and I currently

teach at the graduate level, so I believe that he is well taken care of, academically.

. . . . .

Sabrina,

We share joint custody of W. I am reporting to you plainly that I do not agree to W leaving the established two-hour driving radius to Virginia as you have planned. If you choose to go to Virginia for a reported emergency surgery this is your prerogative. Fortunately we have a wonderful alternative available in Ben and Mary Ellen, and W will not have to be present while Steven undergoes an emergency surgery. Certainly you will want to be available to Steven and not touring military sites.

W has already been taken out of school for what you have considered educational enhancement opportunities. W needs to remain in school and maintain a consistent schedule.

This driving schedule is not appropriate for W.

The reemergence of your claim of molestation [Sean] is telling. How quickly you will move to destroy people. Have you lost all sense of healthy shame?

You didn't respond to my request to honour the Skype breathalyzer testing ordered by the court. Will you agree to honour my request? I am in no way obfuscating here. I believe fully that alcohol is a real issue in your relationship to Steven. You are actually arguing that specialized-even highly specialized-military personnel are immune from alcohol dependency? This would defy the available research, and I would have thought you would be well aware of this reality as a public health professional. Public health professionals too struggle with alcohol

268

dependency. The suggestion that you can't find high performing people and alcoholism together is absurd.

You and Steven are free to drink yourselves into oblivion, but not with my son present. W needs to have the security of a home free of a dependent parent. Certainly you know children will mold behavior around this dynamic to protect a sense of stability. The conspiratorial atmosphere in your home is unnerving. The sudden announcement of this trip is unnerving.

You do agree, I hope, that it was clearly established in the court proceedings that you suffer from alcohol dependency.

You don't suddenly move beyond dependency. This trip has emerged out of nowhere. It has been presented as if it is a forgone conclusion. I am saying I do not support the trip in any way and I have legitimate concerns over my son's wellbeing. Again, W is first here. I am asking you to stop running behind your protective veil of accusation and slander. The onus is on you here. You understand the cycle of dependency, the distortions, obfuscations, twists.

I was surprised by what you wrote about grades and attendance. Apart from the myriad research that links school attendance with academic performance, I am also interested in the school functioning as a stabilizing force in W's life. Daily routine, daily attendance.

W needs to remain with Ben and Mary Ellen. Please provide the pickup details to me so I may then communicate them to Ben and Mary Ellen. I will make sure they have arranged for W. If you take W out of our established two-hour radius I consider you to be in violation of our agreement, and at that point I am doubly concerned from a safety/security perspective. I would then act accordingly.

· · · · ·

Steven has so much more to offer my son than Peter and I believe Peter was desperately trying to prevent that from becoming obvious.

· · · · ·

Peter,

...Steven and I have all necessary documentation ready to go if you plan to move forward. I chose to discontinue this dialogue, which is unproductive. I will be happy to answer any logistical questions and won't respond to any more disparaging remarks/statements. I will send a land line number as soon as I arrive in VA.

This is when my attorney ended it. The next day, I received an email at 10:36 p.m. asking that W spend the day with Ben and Mary Ellen. Peter used the word "you" in a accusatory manner sixteen times.

· · · · ·

Emails of this nature had started to arrive every week. After a string of pages-long emails started arriving every day, I became exhausted and a little depressed. I periodically closed my office door and slept for an hour or so. My job requires quite a lot of concentration and focus. I was so tired, distracted and irritable that I couldn't accomplish anything without taking these naps.

61 HUMPTY DUMPTY—HOW DO I PUT MYSELF BACK TOGETHER?

AT THE END OF NOVEMBER 2012, I posted to my blog:

"I can hardly believe I've wasted so much time affected by someone so sick. I could, if I let myself, sit and cry over so much circular negative energy....waste...of my life. I can't believe I didn't see it earlier and I can't believe I tolerated so much. I can't believe I let my daughters see my mistreatment and disrespect day after day. He offered me emptiness and shame. He did not enhance my life at all. Why didn't I think I could get away and make it on my own? Why didn't I just do it? Now I am stuck for nine more years, dealing with destructive and damaging words, condescension, lies, distortions...stuck...with a sociopath.

Part of the healing process, I learned through court ordered DBT, is radical acceptance of where I am. Of course I am exhausted: his words are meant to tear me down, get a reaction; get me to slip up. Of course I am depressed: he's taken so much, I've lost my daughters, I fear losing my son, I anticipate what's coming next, I am a single mother providing and I need to get my work done, his words are lies and I can't get to rationality or truth. So how do I get out of this? How do I even move with my unavoidable reality?

. . . . .

I bend down and pick up a disgusting napkin that isn't mine because why should the cleaning lady have to do it? I take the vomit soaked rug in my car (my son at that time did get car sick from time to time) and find a bag to put it in and put it in my trunk instead of leaving it at the side of the road. I work on two things today instead of ten and tell myself it's okay. I buy my son a cookie cake for school and take it in to school even though I'm exhausted and depressed and it's hard to get out of bed. I reach out to the community I've created. I breathe deeply and look at the light out of my window. I remember I'm not a prisoner in my home; his words are only words and I am not living with him. I continue to change my thoughts in order to detach my soul from negative messages imbedded deeply. And I remember that I have a note a dear friend wrote, from that long ago small group of women who all meant so much.

· · · · ·

Sabrina,

When you come to mind, I saw white. Blow in the breeze, linen white. Pure fresh white as clean sheets and think white towels white. In fact, I could smell the whiteness--fresh air, grass, linen, sunshine all mixed into the white. Purity of purpose, clarity of sight, a true and clear heart. So white that the sky and grass look bright green and true blue against it. A summer day.

· · · · ·

I didn't accept those words at the time because I lived with a man who was trying to crush my spirit and blacken my soul; I thought I was a disgusting and horrible person. I am slowly accepting that I am not what I was told and continue to be told I am. I will chose to do good, smile even though I don't feel like it, take one minute at a time, remember I have someone who truly loves me, just as I am, slowly get my work done and hug my son. I'll feel better again soon....he won't win...."

62 CHRISTMAS BREAK: CONTAIN AND COMFORT

December 2012

STEVEN AND I WERE ON the same holiday visitation schedule with our sons; we spent the same years together with them and they spent the same years with our exes. This year, neither of us had our children for Christmas, so I flew to Alaska to be with Steven. We had a beautiful time and grew closer than ever, talking about marriage and about having all three boys with us, eventually.

He was still a year and a half away from a potential twenty-year retirement; during his career he had engaged in more than two hundred fifty combat operations and had been awarded the Silver Star and three Bronze Stars, among other honors. At this time, he was living with an undiagnosed traumatic brain injury (TBI), post-traumatic stress disorder (PTSD) and a myriad of other physical ailments—all stemming from what he had done and experienced during his selfless, heroic service, facing the unimaginable. He spent his career saving, rescuing and protecting; the brain that he once controlled, with a psychological strength that most of us cannot fathom, was now betraying him. He was a military elite, viewed as not needing any help, but he really did need help. He counted on my help—without knowing exactly why at this time.

. . . . .

I kept handling interpersonal relationships as if I were a fish out of water—flailing and out of control. A fish must be contained, the hook must be removed and the fish must be placed back into the water by a helping hand for it to find life and peace again. I was not going to make it through all of the trauma and my bad decisions if I didn't have someone to help me. My son's life depended on mine.

. . . . .

Steven and I went out to karaoke and dancing one night during the break. At that time, Steven drove an old Volkswagen Westfalia and when we got in it to drive home, we decided to stay in town and sleep in the van, instead. Winter in Alaska is very cold, but Steven is always prepared. He pulled out a one-person sleeping bag and, holding me tightly, rolled it up and around us. We were fully clothed, my back to him with my head against his chest; he tightly cocooned me with his arms. He kissed me on the top of my head and told me that

276

he loved me. We fell asleep immediately and woke in the exact same position, more than twelve hours later. In that waking moment, I felt contentment and peace while the sun shone brightly into the van; *I realized that this was the greatest human intimacy I had ever experienced.* Steven had contained and comforted me and I had done the same for him. We still talk about our night in the one-person sleeping bag and now we make it a priority to contain and comfort each other, again and again.

63

THE DOMESTIC VIOLENCE "VICTIM" WILL

NOT LEAVE HER "PERPETRATOR" ALONE

THAT SAME CHRISTMAS, JO BEGAN to send emails and we didn't even have the boys. Like Peter, Jo was desperate to keep Steven and I apart; her emails the same threatening, obsessive, living in the past, condescending, exaggerating/lying, and jealous tone. We were sure that she was communicating both with Peter and with Betsy because she knew more information than either of them knew on their own. Jo was passing information back and forth between Peter and Betsy.

. . . . .

On December 30, 2012, Jo sent a five-page single-spaced rant against me, which revealed the information flow. She changes from second to third person regularly in these excerpts. As the email continues, it deteriorates, as if she is losing control of herself.

"...Or maybe it's Steven having his girlfriend out this past summer without telling the boys.

They explicitly told you that they did not want to go to Kentucky to see your girlfriend, Sabrina, and they didn't want to see her period. You dismissed their feelings by telling them that you would talk about it when they got to your dad's house. Then low and behold she shows up with her son (1 of 3 children, 2 daughters of which are not on speaking terms) right as the boys get there, giving them quite a shocking surprise. Then you proceed to take them to Kentucky without telling them or telling me, hiding their phones so they couldn't get help.

Or maybe it was when you bribed them to cut their hair and Sabrina shaved their heads with a dull razor, making them look like kids in a Jewish concentration camp. (It took Jay weeks to recover and the hair dresser couldn't believe the damage that was done to both boys hair.) Or maybe it was Sabrina mentioning vulgar, inappropriate things to the boys in reference to movies, her gay parties, experiences with other woman. Or maybe it was the boxes of wine she drank....... not sure, but I'm willing to bet it was all of these things the boys have mention over time on their own.

Then I was told at random Sabrina's abuse of her two older children. Then I was made aware of some activity that Sabrina told my sister of during a visit to my sister's so the boys could see their cousins. Sabrina mentioned things like: her son sleeping in a closet, her daughters hating her, her gay lifestyle, and so on.....quite alarming.

Because I have had quite an interesting experience recently seeing that Sabrina is being investigated through social services making you, Steven, apparently under the watchful eye as well. I hope to get to the bottom of this of course. Maybe you both could help with that. I am also quite aware of other multiple offenses.

It has occurred to me that the added stress is in relation to Steven's current company staying with him. His girlfriend, Sabrina, is a cause for stress, which I will address later.

This just fueled the fire even more when Steven relayed that he noticed the boys were scared to talk on Sunday, which was not the case.

. . . . .

Steven's boys repeatedly looked up over the computer screen with scared expressions whenever Steven mentioned me or my son and especially if I casually joined him for a Skype session.

. . . . .

Addressing your fiancé and the boys desire to talk to just you, is a reasonable request under the circumstances. It certainly is appropriate for the limited and most deceptive time that they have been forced or tricked into seeing her. Once again, it comes from a culmination of things that have been presented to them and they have verbally expressed to me on their own.

280

....Otherwise, do not harass, threaten or bully me, or Thomas and Jay. We have had enough. Your command has been in continued contact with me and I will not hesitate to inform them of this. Your continued actions are par for the course for me and continue to get worse, but for the boys, they are young and still have hope. It is time to Stop being a part of the problem and start being a part of the solution. Jo.

. . . . .

In other emails, Jo threatens, directly and indirectly, that if Steven allows his children to interact with me, she will withhold communication and visitation (my second book will expand on this). She made false accusations against Steven to authorities, his superiors, friends, family and neighbors, claiming things that shocked him. Before she left Alaska to move to Florida, Jo contacted Steven's Officer in Charge, stating that he was stalking her and watching her. In her emails, Jo threatened documentation and witnesses, but because she is a woman and he was in the military, she was simply believed. His OIC just took her at her word.

64 CLEANING OUT MY CLOSETS

IN APRIL 2013, STEVEN WAS transferred to Virginia Beach. The housing market finally turned around, so I began the process of trying to sell or rent my house so that my son and I could move in with Steven. I gave my renters more than a month's notice, but after that, I lived with tense silences and obvious anger. This was much worse than if they had just talked about their frustration or confronted me. Even yelling at me would've been better. I know that it stunk for them; I felt badly about them having to move again. A few weeks before the move, my toilet leaked and the moisture brought up the pleasant smell of animal urine from years before. Steven paid to re-carpet my entire house. I sold most of what I owned. My brother flew in and packed my ten-foot truck while I sat in court with Peter who was again on the phone, still representing himself. It was both scary and exciting. I had lived in the area for nineteen years; it was the only place my son had ever known. I was able to maintain my faculty position by taking a reduction in hours and pay, teaching my class as a hybrid of both web-based and in-class instruction.

The house was in a deed-restricted community; my neighbors and, therefore, the board were opposing my renting the house. I didn't have any offers to buy, only rent, and I didn't have the resources to float it while I waited to sell. I spent a thousand dollars hiring a real estate attorney to fight the board and explain my situation. The board relented and I was allowed to rent my house for two years.

Along with the upkeep of having the house "showing ready," I packed up my attic. It was, week after week, physically and emotionally exhausting.

. . . . .

In May 2013, I posted to my blog:

"I saved the dresses my girls were photographed in, I saved every worksheet, report card, ballet shoe, dance outfit, every pointe shoe, piano book, favorite baby clothes, pictures, albums, baby books, toys, dolls, room decorations...and now what do I do with all this?

I'm taking it one box at a time...

I sold the Barbies and the doll house toys, some clothes and some room decorations. Things that weren't as sentimental as others. I've sold the living room furniture and other smaller furniture. I'm still paying attorney fees so I'm selling everything I can.

Today I began the photo albums and miscellaneous awards and papers. I found dozens of cards and notes to me. I found notes from Peter thanking me for bringing the girls into the world and taking such good care of them. I should have gone through this prior to the divorce trial when I was accused of the exact opposite.

But here I am reading and remembering my life with my girls. It was hard, but I loved being with them. They brought me tremendous joy and love.

Here are a few of my favorites:

Dear Ma, I love you, ur the greatest ma alive. You are always supportive of me. Thanks for offering kind and gentle words to me. You are wonderful...

You have been a great mother! You still are a great mother! You are such an amazing mom. You even cared about me during your doctorite (and that's hard, because a doctorite is hard). You know what you are? Your warm, you are fun, your my whole sunshine. I love you! XXxOoOXOxoXx (ask for explanation).

A card "The beautiful center of our family."

Dear Mom, Like the card said, you are the center of our family. Happy Birthday P.S. I hope you like your present.

Dear Mom you are a genius at work but a lover at home. Happy Birthday

And that's what your famous for!

I love you, You are my very best Mom. You are my friend. You are we, I love you better than anything! I love you with my heart.

Dear Mom,
Because you were here you've been a role model. Also you've helped me be more confident about myself. You do just the right things a mom should do. You do not embrass me because I'm not afriad to say "that's my mom over there!" Also you let me express myself through ballet and art. It always makes me feel good when you say I did awesome on my dance. Yours truly...

Dear Mommy, I love you very very very much! I missed you so much. I hated being away from you. I never ever want you to leave.

. . . . .

And now we are apart and I hope they're ok. It would be hard to live without a mother. I hope....they see me in their past...sometimes. Mine is FILLED with them.

285

I miss my girls so much.

. . . . .

While cleaning out my attic, I found a journal I kept when my oldest daughter was born. I was just over two months into my 20th year. Although I was very young and had to have the nurse show me how to change a diaper, I wrote pages about how much I loved her; how overjoyed I was to hold her and watch her. I carefully documented her birth, her every move and every development.

Jan 14, 1991 "...I can hear you stirring in the bassinet at the end of the bed, it's 1:42 a.m. and I'm wondering when you'll wake up for your feeding. I miss you and can't wait to hold you close to me. You're my little girl and I love you so much. I hope you'll always love me back..."

Jan 25, 1991 "I've already gone back to work at PASS (an after school program)...It is almost unbearable to leave you, I hate it."

And then July 1993 my entries stopped. The next and last entry was completely different.

June 22, 1994 "It's been a long time honey, I'm sorry. I'm sorry for sleeping in the mornings. You are such a good girl....."

. . . . .

Looking back, it's clear what happened. At the beginning, my essence was still bubbling forth; I had taken to motherhood, wholeheartedly, accepting my unexpected role as if there was no other path for me. But within a few short years, my organic generally positive, happy and outgoing individuality had been altered within a controlling and fear-based union. I had become depressed and had begun my slow, methodical decent toward the edge of sanity and insanity.

Many scientific journal articles include psychological aggression (behaviors that are non-violent but are intended to increase or maintain control over the victim) as intimate partner violence. These behaviors include insults and name-calling, restriction of victim's contact with friends and family, isolation and financial abuse.

"Women with a history of IPV face severe health consequences, including poor mental health...depression, anxiety, poor social functioning, poor physical health, increased substance use, and increased frequency of chronic disease, chronic mental illness, and injury compared to women without histories of IPV [16]."

I went through nearly a dozen wheels for my girls' wagon, pulling and pushing to every free service or food bank.....a scavenger.

Peter's answer was to ask for money from family. He was not compelled to take responsibility himself; it was always someone else's fault and responsibility for our poverty.

In an email from Peter at the end of March 2013, where he justifies not paying support for my son, Peter says this: "I don't have any excess cash. I put my money toward raising two daughters solely…"

The daughters he "is raising" are ages nineteen and twenty-two. So he is providing for two young women as if spouses. He took no financial responsibility for his real spouse and those same daughters when young, ironically, when they needed him most. Only when they became young women did he chose to put his money toward them. The circle is not a little mind-blowing. At one of my son's baseball games last year, a friend leaned over to me and said, "it looks like Peter found someone else; maybe he'll leave you alone now." I looked and turned to her sadly and said, "that's my daughter, not his girlfriend," and to see the look on her face made me feel even more helpless.

. . . . .

I stayed too long and tolerated too much. I betrayed myself and my daughters. I was scared of so many things…..

Dear Precious Daughters,

It's been a long time, I'm sorry. I'm sorry for sleeping through 2 decades. I'm sorry for all of the pain I caused you. I'm sorry for being so ugly at times, allowing my own frustration at my situation to burst out at you. You are such good girls...."

65 MOVING IN WITH STEVEN

STEVEN AND I ELOPED ON June 21, 2013 in order to avoid any hindrance to moving my son in with us and to live as a married couple, not just co-habiting. My son and I were staying with Steven and his two sons for the beginning of summer break. I went back to Kentucky with my son after Steven and I were married, to be heard before our family court Judge. Summer break visitation had yet to be determined; it seemed to be an afterthought for Peter, something the Judge mentioned. The Judge, as always, asked if I had heard from my daughters. I had the opportunity to relay the tragic Christmas story of John and Peter Walton, and of the damage done to my son.

. . . . .

During Easter weekend, Peter sent threatening emails to me about eventually taking my son, as he had already taken my girls. He owed thousands of dollars in child support. I feared that he would kidnap my son and I could envision Peter pontificating as he did so often, "what would be in his best interest would be to stay here with me." What was different this time is that I knew that I didn't have to accept the fear; I filed an Emergency Protective Order and it was granted. The Waltons eluded the service of the order. Peter was out of the country. Still, his brother Ben could be served and be asked to communicate the notice. On several occasions, Ben was not at home to accept service.

Peter could not take our son out of the United States until the EPO was served and he appeared in court. By the time Peter appeared in court and cleared things up, he had the possibility of only a little more than two weeks for time share. The Judge ordered that if Peter did not have his son at the designated drop off location at the exact agreed upon time, there would be a warrant for his arrest.

In order for the EPO to be dropped, Peter could not communicate with me again, outside of email or text, unless it was an emergency. He was ordered to not bring up anything from the past and to stay focused on the present, and on only logistics about our son.

· · · · ·

The Judge had recognized Peter's PAS and had restricted visitation to a point that was comfortable and appropriate. There were court-ordered boundaries, restricting his communication with me. It was Peter's responsibility to change any timeshare or initiate visitation/communication with my son. The court recognized him for who he really was.

66 COPS AT THE CRACK HOUSE

STEVEN'S HOME IN VIRGINIA BEACH was still occupied by renters, so we rented another house from one of his colleagues. We called it "the crack house" because there would be sketchy individuals and cops outside most nights. Jo, apparently, researched the area and then notified attorneys that we had the children staying in a house across from a registered sex offender. As it was, we did not let the boys go outside without us. We didn't have furniture because I had sold mine and the military was holding on to Steven's until we could move into our house.

· · · · ·

We returned to "the crack house" after a day at the local water park and dinner out. Steven's dad and stepmother had come for a visit and were staying at a nearby hotel. They visited with us for a while, at the house, and left at around 10:00 p.m. After I put my son to bed, Steven's boys stayed up to watch a movie with us. When Jo called, the boys went up to their room to talk with her.

She required that they take calls away from anyone else. She interrogated them and didn't want us to overhear; the Judge in Steven and Jo's custody suit identified this tendency in her and ordered her to stop the behavior—stating that it was unhealthy for the boys. Steven listened at the door and, when he determined that yet another interrogation was happening, he told the boys to come downstairs, that there was no reason for them to take the call upstairs. Suddenly, Jay ran into the downstairs bathroom and locked the door. I knew exactly what was happening—Jo was setting us up. I banged on the door and when Jay refused to open it, I told Steven to take it off the hinges. By then, Jay was screaming "help me, help me!" Steven got the door open, took the phone from him and hung up. Steven had the boys sit down and I said, "the police will be here soon and all of you could be taken from us, including my son." Everyone was quiet and I said, "she is definitely calling the police and I need to let them know the backstory." So I called. The following is the transcript from that call.

```
CHIQ   PAGE NO.0001 1531   ADM2   09-20-2013 16:27
                    VA BEACH LAW CALLS FOR SERVICE TRAN
                    CALLS-FOR-SERVICE INQUIRY RESPONSE

---------------------------------------------------------------------
INITIATE:   23:03:29 07-19-2013   CALL NUMBER:       132001347
ENTRY:      23:05:21              CURRENT STATUS:  CLOSED
DISPATCH:   23:09:27              PRIMARY UNIT:    428B
ON SCENE:   23:13:28              JURISDICTION     P
CLOSE:      23:47:13              DISPOSITION:     N

LOCATION:  835 CRASHAW ST  ,  ( COLERIDGE CT & CAMPION AV )
DAREA:     4TH
BEAT:      428
RD:        458016                 TYPE:     DOMS
FIRE:      HF379J                 PRIORITY: 2

CP:   MS BROWN
ADDRESS:
PHONE:     ▓▓▓▓▓▓▓▓▓▓▓▓

07-19-2013
23:05:21 ST2  ENTRY     TEXT:COMPL STATES HER KIDS ARE HERE IN VB WITH HER EXHUSB
                        AND AND HIS GF..COMPL STATES HER ●YO SON CALLED HER AND
                        LEFT THE LINE OPEN SO COMPL COULD HERE GF YELLING AT HER
                        11YO SON..THE ●YO LOCKED HIMSELF IN THE BATHROOM.. \NAME
                        :MS BROWN \PH: ▓▓▓▓▓▓▓▓▓ , (MTF)
23:05:54 P4   HOLD
23:06:54 ST2  SUPP      TEXT:COMPL STATES THAT SHE COULD HER YOUNGEST STAING HE J
                        UST WANTED SOME MEDICINE FOR HIS EARS..COMPL STATED THAT
                        HER SON WAS STATING HE IS SCARED OF THEM..THE COMPL WOULD
                        LIKE FOR OFCRS TO GO..COMPL STATED SHE COULD (MTF)
23:07:26 ST2  UPDATE    TYPE:ASTC-->DOMS DTYPE:AST CITIZEN-->DOMESTIC
23:07:26 ST2  SUPP      TEXT:HERE BOTH KIDS GETTING YELLED AT BY THE ADULTS AND T
                        HEN THE LINE DISCONNECTED
23:07:57 ST2  UPDATE    PRI:3-->2
23:07:57 ST2  SUPP      TEXT:COMPL STATES THIS IS AN ONGOING ISSUE..THIS OCCURED
                        WITHIN 10 MIN..
23:08:35 P4   HOLD
23:09:27 P4   DISPATCH  427C 427B
23:09:27 P4   ID        427C  ▓▓▓▓)BUCK,JUSTIN S
23:09:27 P4   ID        427B (▓▓▓▓)SHELTON,JONATHAN P.
23:09:29 ST2  SUPP      TEXT:COMPLS EXHUSBAND IS STEVEN BROWN..W/ DARK HAIR BLUE
                        EYES 6'0 TALL...COMPL STTAES THE SUBJ IS A NAVY SEAL AND
                        HAS ALOT OF WEAPONS..THE FEMALE IS SABRINA WALSH..W/F RED
                        HAIR MAYBE 5'4..COMPL STATES THAT THEY ARE ALWAYS DRINKI
                        NG..
23:09:56 P4   ENROUTE   427C
23:09:56 P4   ENROUTE   427B
23:10:21 P4   BACK-ER   427B 428B
23:10:21 P4   ID        428B (▓▓▓▓)HAMANN,PAUL E
23:11:18 ST2  SUPP      TEXT:COMPL STATES THAT SHE HAS FULL CUSTODY OF THE KIDS..
                        THE MALE HAS VISITATION..THE COMPL IS IN FLORIDA..COMPL S
                        TATED THAT THE KIDS ARE TOLD NOT TO CALLL THE COMPL AND T
                        HREATENS TO HIT THE CHILDREN IF THEY CALL THE COMPL..
23:11:51 ST2  SUPP      TEXT:CPS HAS BEEEN INVESTIGATING THE MALE SUBJ IN FLORIDA
                        ..

CHIQ   PAGE NO.0002 1531   ADM2   09-20-2013 16:27
                    VA BEACH LAW CALLS FOR SERVICE TRAN
                    CALLS-FOR-SERVICE INQUIRY RESPONSE

23:13:18 ST2  SUPP      TEXT:COMPL WOULD LIKE IF OFCRS WOULD CONTACT HER BY PHONE
                        TO LET HER KNOW OF HER CHILDRENS WELFARE..CAN BE REACHED
                        AT ▓▓▓▓▓▓▓▓
23:13:28 P4    ONSCENE  427B
23:14:20 V492  ONSCENE  428B
```

Page 1

```
Printed for: ADM2/1531                                    Fri Sep 20 16:31:23 2013
23:14:25 V602 ONSCENE  427C
23:15:00 ST2  MISC     .1347, COMPL JUST STATED THAT HER EXHUSBAND HIDES THE ALC
                       OHOL..THE COMPL STATED SHE COULD HER THE FEMALE YELLING A
                       T THE KIDS COME OUT OF THERE YOUR GOING TO GET US INTO TR
                       OUBLE WITH CPS AGAIN
23:16:43 S3   MISC     .1347, SABRINA BROWN /#859.285.7271 CALLING FROM INSIDE W
                       ORRIED THAT THE CHILDS BIOLOGICAL MOTHER WOULD CALL THE C
                       OPS ON THEM. SHE ADVSD THE CHILDS MOTHER WAS ON THE PHONE
                       WITH COMPS STEPSON, AND THE MOTHER TOLD THE SON TO LOCK
                       HIMSELF IN THE BATHROOM AND CONVINCED HIM TO BE SCARED. S
                       ABRINA SAID SHE WANTED AN OFFICER TO COME TO THE HOUSE TO
                       INTERVIEW THE CHILDREN AND CHECK THE CONDITIONS SO PD CA
                       N SEE FOR THEMSELVES EVERYTHING IS OK. I ADVSD SABRINA PO
                       LICE WERE ALREADY ONSCENE OF HER HOUSE.
 23:41:13 V602 ONSCENOK 427B
 23:41:13 V602 ONSCENOK 428B
 23:41:13 V602 ONSCENOK 427C
 23:44:30 V602 INSRVICE 427C
 23:45:33 V425 INSRVICE 427B
 23:47:10 P4   MISC     428B, PLS CLR, NR. NO INDICATIONS THAT ANY BODY WAS UNDER
                        THE INFLUENCE OF ALCOHOL. SPOKE WITH BOTH OF THE BOYS, ██
                        ████████████, SEPERATELY FROMT THE ADULTS, BOTH DENIED B
                        EING MISTREATED OR NOT PROVIDED WITH PROPER TREATMENT. SP
                        OKE WITH THE COMPL VIA ██████ PHONE, SHE REITERATED WHAT S
                        HE HAD TOLD CALL TAKER. I ASSURED HER EVERYTHING WAS WELL
                        AT CS LOCATION. TKS[07/19/13234710001]
 23:47:13 P4   CLEAR    428B N
 23:47:13 P4   CLOSE    428B N

OPERATOR ASSIGNMENTS:       ST2  ███    STALCH,AMBER M.
                            P4   ███    WESTBY,PATRICIA A
                            V492 ███    HAMANN,PAUL E
                            V602 ███    BUCK,JUSTIN S
                            S3   ███    SANSONE,JONATHAN
                            V425 ███    SHELTON,JONATHAN P.
AS OF 07-19-2013-23:47:10   P4   ███    ASPER,TIA

**** REPORT COMPLETED ****
```

Jay's ear was bothering him and Steven prepared to do a peroxide treatment on him, something the SEALS do all the time. Steven already had it out and ready. The police officers, after interviewing the children, told us that it was good that I had called and even offered to help in the future, if there were more false allegations. Having been told by Jo that Steven was a dangerous Navy SEAL, the police had surrounded the house with lights out, and approached the scene at a high threat level, as if he was armed, dangerous and intoxicated. It could have been traumatic for all of us— even more than it already was.

I called Steven's stepmother to tell her what happened. She said, "but everything was fine and everyone happy when we left." I said, "that's typical of Jo, especially because everything was fine." She said, "I can hear how upset you are in your voice; your voice is shaking." I said, "this is our life, it will not stop with her." I was glad that they had seen how detached Jo was from reality and how her interference was damaging all of us. Maybe things would be okay again with them, now that they saw first-hand what we were up against.

. . . . .

This episode was disconcertingly familiar to the one I'd had with my middle daughter when Peter called the police. When court officials, social services or police are called to a scene, there is no sure outcome; anything could happen. Because of Jo, I had been so dangerously close to losing my son. That night, Steven and I had our first conversation about whether or not it was in anyone's best interest to have more visitation with his sons. Jo's interferences were that bad—for everyone.

67 WHO AM I AFTER ALL OF THIS?

I POSTED TO MY BLOG in September 2013:

"I loved to be outside with my brothers. We just loved the outside. We always lived in the country so we didn't have many friends to play with outside—just ourselves. Growing up, with limited income, we played with mom-made milk carton blocks, Barbies, matchbox cars, imaginary play, we mostly played outside. My son is just like we were; sun up to sun down outside playing.

When I was in elementary school I imagined flying above everyone else in line for the cafeteria and being above all the difficulties and misfortunes that haunt children then and today. In middle school, I was a sixty pound, red headed, freckled face, awkward girl. I was filled with insecurities, anxieties and un-comfortableness with my changing body and mind. I always felt different, awkward and always hiding from shame.

But... I also had an adventurous side. The older of my brothers and I would often do something we called "creeking" (We grew up in upstate New York with an abundance of water sources). This meant that we would put on old jeans and sneakers and head to nearby waterfalls. We would spend most of the day going up stream against the current, sometimes in water above our chests. We would sometimes slip under the water and the current would take us until we could maintain footing on slippery, mossy rocks. Those were some of the best and most exciting days of my life. I loved summer creeking days; often walking along the edge of an at least three story high water fall. There I was confident, stable, strong and grounded both mentally and physically.

My brother and I also loved to climb all over the roof of our old farm house. I remember sitting straight up on the highest peak looking over the edge to the front lawn—I could see the top branches of the fully grown oak trees in our front lawn at eye level.

What happened to me that I would have a devastatingly incapacitating fear of heights? Fear of people, of situations; fear of what might happen, what might currently be happening.

The past summer (at the crack house) I had gone to a water park. I hated even the steps up to the slide. All day I was lovingly badgered by my companions to go down the scariest slide. I began to "work up to it." I thought back to my creeking days and wondered why this was so damn hard. It was a ten foot straight drop and then sharp turns. The slide began in an enclosed case with the sound of a beating heart. I wanted so much to bravely conquer this unnatural (for me) fear. I got into the chamber and told myself to just keep breathing through the seconds of free fall. I was in a full panic by the time the floor dropped out from under me. The next thing I realized I was underwater and thought, really? They fill the tubes with water for further torment? As I came to my senses…. I was at the bottom and could get out. I did it. I survived. I did it again just to be sure.

. . . . .

Physical and emotional abuse, especially by someone promising to care and love, affects the external environment as well. A horse freely running one day might, after being beaten for years, repeatedly, fear leaving the stall of a barn. We sink into smaller places as our emotional and physical stability is robbed. Our freedom, our bravery, our ability to understand how our physical bodies will react in the environment is stolen. I have, systematically, put myself into situations I fear to practice freedom. I'll get back on those roof tops."

68 LIVING WITH PTSD

I RESEARCH VIOLENT DEATHS AS part of my career. I have done this for more than fifteen years, which is the main reason that my daughters gave for finding Peter's abuse of me hard to believe. They think that if I was exposed to the scientific side of this issue for so long, then I would've seen what was happening and ended things long before I did. Unfortunately, though a professional in the field, I maintained a naiveté in my personal life, one that I am embarrassed to articulate.

In April 2014, I posted to my blog:

"I live with the after effects of being abused by isolation. Like a victim being thrown back into a "normal" existence while feeling like an alien, I too, can revert back to my abusive state and, nearly in a literal fetal position, go into my own mind and live there. It's not depression, it's close to catatonic (which interestingly falls under PTSD in the DSM). I learned to live for over two decades in my own mind. I had no way of experiencing genuine exposure while with Peter. I learned to go inside and be comfortable only there. While in this warped state of mind I can only be engaged for a few hours a day. I have been here for over a week now.

On the flip side, I am healing from PTSD from my relationship with a sociopath. So what triggered me? I....am....feeling....everything....everything.....and some of it hurts...a lot....I'm not feeling with anger, I am feeling with sadness.

. . . . .

I have read narratives of violence for my whole career and it has been a distant story, like a TV show or movie—just numbers—and I've been criticized for this—for being callous in presentations. I am working on a three part series with the Centers for Disease Control and Prevention on child homicide deaths in our nation. Today, I cried. Tears ran down my face.... for mostly the second and third and fourth children that were killed, generally by their parents. What horror to watch and wait without the adult knowledge to act. The setting them on fire and the sexual assaults...real stories. Story after story. I don't feel good, I feel unsettled, I feel lonely, I have isolated myself, but what did they feel? Maybe by allowing myself to be in this state, I can tell their stories in a way that will be an honor to their short lives. Those dear little people, who died because their parents became consumed with emotion beyond their capabilities. I believe they each had a guardian angel that covered them with their wings as they passed out of this world. This world that can be so terrible.

· · · · ·

I have learned something. I am dealing with these triggers as I once was conditioned, but tomorrow I will spend more time engaged and the next day a little more. I can re-train my mind. I will learn to see and process pain without reverting back to the safe inward world I have created. God bless me as I step out from under rose colored glasses and see the world as it is...even when it hurts so much my body trembles."

69 A RESPONSE FROM A DEAR FRIEND

THIS IS A RESPONSE TO that blog post from a friend, who both literally and figuratively walked with me through my chapter of "My Worst Fears:"

"Your naïveté existed before as a coping mechanism. It is cracking. You are beginning to see, you don't need it anymore. Because you have survived your own horrors, you know deep down, you will survive this. Because you have survived, you will understand. Because you have sought justice in your own life, you will help others find the justice they need. Because you have sought justice, you can take off those rose colored glasses. See through your former naïveté. Rest gentle, find shelter and joy in the love you have found in your life. You have worked so hard. You have come so far. I have watched some of this transformation. You have tools to help you survive this harsh reality now. So come out and see this world you've worked so hard to make for yourself.

It's a self-preservation mechanism. It's easy to get triggered when you see things like what you see involving domestic violence. But you have done so much wonderful work to make your life a safe place to live, both for you and your family. You don't need to hide. You can come out now. Share with the ones you've learned are safe to let in. Lean on them. Let in their light. I love you more than I can show, as far away as I am living. If I could, I would love to take you to coffee. I would love to give you a big, reassuring hug. This is all I can do. I'm holding you up to the Light of the Universe right now. Love you today and always.. I'll be thinking of you."

70 BLOG EXCHANGES: A QUESTION

IN DECEMBER 2012, I POSED a question on my blog:

"We can't know the mind of a sociopath because it is such an unnatural way to think and behave. So I pose this question, in an effort to understand the mind of a sociopath, to those who have dealt with one. Marriage to one reveals the most because in trying to get away the deepest darkness is revealed, but there are other relationships to sociopaths that might also shed light.

Do you think that, as they outright lie and distort reality, they truly convince themselves that what they are saying is the truth? That they say it so passionately and with such certainty that they begin to really believe what they are saying? Or, over time do they test certain phrases and behaviors and learn that they can push buttons with various people to get what they want? Do they knowingly manipulate; they pull a string and the marionettes move exactly as they've dictated?"

71 BLOG EXCHANGES: RESPONSES

"A: A FRIEND POINTED ME in the direction of your blog today and I just wanted to tell you...thank you.

I am sitting here in tears as I read the things you are writing...because you are writing about MY life experiences. I truly can relate to every single thing you have written so far...and this is the first time in my life that I have heard from someone else who has to deal with it. It brings me to a place of huge anxiety (I too have diagnosed PTSD...) but also it is a huge comfort to know that I'm not alone.

I really just wanted to thank you for sharing your story and your struggles...because nobody else seems to get it. I'm just supposed to get over it and not let it affect me in their eyes. It's a constant battle. We have a son together. And we have joint custody...sort of...just enough to give him zero responsibility and all of the control he wants to have over my life.

Me: It is very scary dealing with these people...VERY!! You have made my day and encourage me to continue what I'm doing. I want to provide support for people like us in so many ways..I wish I could do this full time. There are so many of us and so afraid to talk, and maybe embarrassed, if we can even figure out what is going on...

A: A few years ago I had a "nervous breakdown" of sorts. I started therapy, was out of work for several months while trying out several different medications. The psychiatrist I saw (not my counselor) told me I had PTSD and severe depressive and anxiety disorder. The PTSD was a result of many things...childhood and forward. I apparently fit a profile of a victim quite well...which I hate and I am trying hard to change. And of course, my ex likes to throw that entire experience in my face whenever he can. I'm not on any medications now but still battle the anxiety and depression constantly. I have Tourette Syndrome too...which only complicates my situation. There are days when I would probably not get out of bed if it were not for my son.

Me: I have a theory that sociopaths seek us out. There is so little information out there, don't you think? And with all of our stories so similar you would think there would be by now...

A: There is almost no information out there. And nobody is willing to point their fingers and call someone a sociopath, but they are everywhere. I have huge trust issues with people now, and mostly do not trust myself to be a stronger, wiser person "next time." Hence, I have not had any serious relationships since our breakup...which is going on over 5 years now! I would rather be alone than in a relationship where I am vulnerable again. And I see myself still the way he wanted me to see myself. I hate that he still controls my life in that way. It is a slooowww process. I'm getting there. And I'm not unhappy by any means...I try to find joy in what I have right now...my health and my career and my son. I have much to be thankful for.

Me: We do have a lot to be thankful for! A good friend of mine is still trying to get away and has been for years. He is a pastor and the entire community is against her. Well said, "I see myself still the way he wanted me to see myself," very well said. What a battle to change our self-image!!! I fight it every day.

I have thankfully found someone, and after him telling me hundreds of times "I am not your ex-husband" and continually affirming me, I am taking the risk to love and trust. Night and day difference between relationships, to say the very least. People hurt us and often people can heal us. Don't give up.

B: Maybe this is something to write about, I don't know....But how do I protect my two daughters from marrying someone like Peter? Did your parents see him as a "good Christian boy"? A "pastor's son" so he must be amazing! How will I recognize the signs of my girls dating someone like that? How do I approach them about it?

Just thoughts I was having today. :) I almost ended up with a person like this too. Thankfully he broke up with me for something better! Otherwise I would have followed his abusive ass around for years!

Me: First, you and your husband seem to be on the same team so you'll be united in seeing and dealing with any issues. Stick together and parent together. I've heard that from professionals. And if the boy is too good to be true, he most likely is.

There was much less out there when I was fifteen and met Peter and he and his family were good at pretending. I have to give my family a big break because I was relentless in my defense of Peter and he was too good to be true. He wasn't true at all; he was veneer.

My parents, brothers, sisters-in-laws are heartbroken and angry that they were also taken in by Peter from the beginning. They didn't see it at the time because we protect them, defend them and are always trying to help them. There are signs from the very beginning that are subtle but there.

1. They are unusually attentive and aware of everything you do. They want to be with you as much as possible and begin to become involved in what you are involved in. This may seem flattering, but it's control.

2. Extremely jealous when you spend time with other people, same sex or opposite. Again, this may seem flattering, but it's control. And yet they talk about attributes of the opposite sex and almost make you chase after perfection. They will give you just enough compliments to keep you around, but keep you unsettled at the same time. As teenagers this physical insecurity is a particularly sensitive area. They cheat on you from the very beginning. Whatever they can get away with. Also, to keep you on edge

they flippantly break up with you, and devastate you, and then just when you've moved on, they are back.

3. Your circle of friends starts to shrink and keeps shrinking the longer you date. *I think this is the biggest red flag*

4. They try to lock you down with some sort of formal commitment. For example: marriage, pregnancy, geography (a move). My oldest daughter started dating a potential abuser and he was talking marriage (and his family) in her junior year in high school. Also he would constantly comment on actresses. One night he "playfully" tripped her and then laughed...She is no longer with him, thankfully. Trying to get her away from him was probably the worst we ever fought as mother and daughter (I made a lot of mistakes).

5. They highlight any family problems, mental illness or physical illness and make themselves "your healer," "protector," "get you away from problems."

6. They seem to have a private agenda—a drama—that makes them needy.

7. Start to tell you what to wear or to cut your hair/grow it out, I think to see how far they can go.

8. They have anger and disrespect for other females.

9. While we dated Peter was known for fighting. His senior picture revealed a black eye from a fight the previous night. He was quick to get that angry. He didn't get angry at me until after we were married, but while we dated he was an overall angry person. There was a picture hanging over a hole in the wall in the

Walton home, which is a great example of how his parents han-dled him. They overlooked EVERYTHING. Peter and his brothers did whatever they wanted; their parenting style was that they would figure it out in the end. After we were married and had our first daughter (we were both still in college) Peter chose to play intramural hockey. I was standing at the sidelines with my daughter in my arms and Peter began to disagree with a friend on the opposing team. Soon Peter was beating him and he was much smaller than Peter. Several people had to calm him down and he was banned from intramurals. We always had holes in walls etc. in our homes. Peter also mistreated animals at a very young age. We knew each other as children and Peter had a reputation, as young as preteen, of being dangerous, mys-terious and a bully.

10. Peter disrespected his mother. He talked to her in a demeaning and belittling way. None of the Walton men respected her, they thought she was dumb and interrupted her, embarrassed, when she tried to join in the conversation at the dinner table.

C: I am overwhelmed by your response! Overwhelmed! I am coming to the realization that the boyfriend in high school was a sociopath! OMG! I knew he was controlling, I knew that he made my friend circle super small even forcing me to choose between my best friend and him, he was violent (but I would say, he didn't hit me just walls, flipping over his sister's swing set). OMG! I just can't believe it!

When I went through counseling a few years ago, my therapist said that he was abusive and I said no. Still after all these years and having a great guy I still didn't think so. She argued and said he was and I should thank God that he dumped me. He did dump me, take me back, get a new girlfriend, take me back, etc. Wow!

At a wedding a few years ago my aunt was commenting on how wonderful my husband is to me and for me. She said, "Remember…? I always thought he was so controlling and wasn't right for you". She was one of my favorite aunts and never said anything because she didn't say unkind things about people but she knew!! This is all connecting right now for me! Thank you!!

D: I by no means am a trained professional. I also can't be sure that this person is a sociopath but there is definitely something wrong with the person I am thinking about. I think that "he" in this circumstance you explained believes that it is reality! I think that it starts as a lie in his head but he works it over and over in his mind until it becomes reality. He also gets others to believe his reality further confirming this lie, in his mind. It's so frustrating! It's like talking to a brick wall!! Like I said, I'm not sure he is a sociopath but he is definitely narcissistic and has some sort of mental illness.

I was wondering, and maybe you will address this in your blog, did Peter have affairs (I think you said he did). If yes, did he stalk and abuse his other ladies? Also why do your girls believe what he says is true? As a woman, how can they tolerate their mother being abused? Just some questions I have had as I've read along with your blog. I appreciate so much what you have shared!

Me: I always knew narcissism ran in the Walton family, but it wasn't until I wanted out of the relationship that I realized it was way beyond that. In your case, what you're looking for is being a victim all the time, no ability to empathize and being miserable. Yes, a brick wall, they cannot hear anything especially anything negative about themselves.

Yes, affairs and with Peter there were other issues, but he didn't feel guilt so anything was difficult to detect. I'm not sure about him stalking any others, I think I might be the only one with that privilege.

My girls...it's the biggest heartbreak. The Waltons all distort anything I try. If I don't talk to them, I'm neglecting them, if I do, I'm harassing them...Peter, and all of them, have made me out to be such an awful person and that's the only messages they are hearing, they both seem fairly isolated still and they aren't hearing my voice at all. ...He also talked about "my mental illness" all the time with them. So over time they didn't think much of me at all. The oldest surprises me because she and I were always very close; the middle Peter continues to have an inappropriate relationship...it's very hard to not be able to do anything about it. They grew up with this man and he presented as the calm, together parent, with all the answers, and they don't know differently. Just like me when we started to date. I think it will take them crossing him and him treating them like he did me. It's sad for my son because he misses them and doesn't understand why they hate me so much.

E: I am currently divorcing and trying to co-parent with a sociopath. I supported him for the past three years while he refused to get a job and I still did all the things at home that a stay at home mom would even though he was there all day. Then when I finally filed for divorce he tried to portray me as mentally unstable, an alcoholic and him as an involved stay at home dad. Luckily both my girls and the judge saw through him. Thanks for your post and keep reaching for the light, I promise it's there!

Me: I have often wondered what he did all day? Have you figured it out? I have suspected watching television.... Do you have any suggestions about "co-parenting?" I'm so happy to hear your girls saw through him. At least I haven't lost my son. In emails responding to my blog I find it's about half and half in regard to custody; a lot of sad stories about losing small children and adult children. I hope he will move on every day. If not for my son, I would never speak to him again.

E: Co-parenting with a sociopath is kind of an ironic term. Our family therapist suggested I read the *Sociopath Next Door* and *Without Conscience* just to get a better understanding of what I am dealing with. It is a careful dance for sure. I just make sure the kids are ok and have a cell phone so they can call me anytime when he starts acting crazy and I have to log every detail of mine and his interactions in case we have to go back to court. He already has a new victim (I mean girlfriend) so that has taken some of the focus off harassing me. I just have to resign myself to the fact that the cost of leaving him is having to deal with his games for the next eight years or until the girls finally have had enough and tell him they don't want to see him anymore--which could very well happen. Maybe I will write a book when I finally get it figured out!

F: Your blog has captured my attention for sure. I can relate to much of what you have experienced and find myself dealing with many of the same types of challenges. Thanks for sharing your stories. Sociopaths are very intelligent and manipulative, and certainly use any bit of information against their victims. I learned that the hard way. It's very easy to lose yourself in the midst of a sociopath. In everything you read about a sociopath, I find it curious that your story is the first I can compare to where children were used to take sides with the sociopath. That is something that should be documented as a typical behavior from a sociopath. I have believed it is because that is truly their level of emotional maturity and they can easily manipulate children. I will keep reading. I feel like for the first time, I am not alone. Thank You!

G: I have been married to my husband for twenty yrs. He is mean to our children and spends no time with our two boys. I went to see a psychologist and she told me after brief conversation about him what his problem was. I have heard of the word but never knew the definition.

Me: I find this interesting because Peter did not want a son, he wanted another daughter. I believe this is because of the father/daughter relationship and it being easier to manipulate daughters. It is known to any of us who are on the other side of our teenage years that there is a period of time where the relationship between a teenage girl and mother is strained and difficult. And to be with a man who was constantly triangulating and putting me in the child role made my relationships nearly impossible. Peter took normal mother/teenage daughter issues and created an impossible wall to surmount.

H: The hard part is confronting him. I have tried many times to tell him I was unhappy but he always managed to talk me into staying and that he would change. Only to go right back to the way he was.

Me: I find myself talking to woman and men in various, and sometimes surprising settings, about sociopaths. At an airport recently a woman told me about a story of her husband of over twenty years. She had four children, he wanted five; she didn't want the fifth and was asking for a divorce. For a month he treated her as he always should, connecting, being loving, and treating her as precious; he was romantic and kind. She softened. After about a month, he turned to her one night and said, "That is done, I just wanted you to know I could do it, but choose not to because you don't deserve to be treated that way." She holds three jobs and cares for the children when she gets home. She's exhausted and doesn't know what to do; she is afraid of a nasty divorce and losing her children.

318

He threatens to present as the perfect and attentive stay at home dad. Oh, I forgot to mention, he chooses to not work one hour outside of the home. So he is threatening that he would take the children, stating that he would be the best to care for the children since that's what he's already doing....the same story over and over.....

I: I'm reading your blog and thinking WOW..pretty much the same situation for me. But only mental and verbal abuse for me--that's enough! It is so frustrating dealing with this. And nobody believes me. My husband, loved by all, I'm the crazy one.....AND he is making me out like the one with the problems. I do admit that I started this process after I realized that I don't have to take this anymore. I was so beaten down and I thought I was a worthless person (lots and lots of examples of things he has said to me) and ...I did contact my first love so that makes me look like I am the horrible person....this is awful and I'm scared too.

Me: What is a person supposed to do when they go years without even the lowest level of human decency much less getting any sort of emotional need met? You are not a horrible person. We, as humans, need to connect to each other and when you're living with a hollow shell of course you were vulnerable and of course you would look for someone with whom you had connected with. Unfortunately, they wait for us to "fail" and then take full advantage. I have been trying to not be so hard on myself. I was desperate for an emotional connection, not knowing what it looked or felt like. I mistook intimacy and validation with receiving attention and being used over and over. Then Peter also used relationships against me so I was in a vicious circle damaging myself further and helping Peter damage me. You are not alone.

J: I feel like crying as I read some of these. It's as if you've been living my life, and you have the words to explain it as I can't. His tone, his condescension, the false accusations, the embellishment, the false concern..... And I've been trying to get the divorce since...

K: The strange thing about sociopathy are the subtleties and physiology that are not aggressive enough to actually have these diseased people committed...this extreme mental chasm cannot be rectified with any amount of therapy. It's a part of the human condition and will be with us forever ....I suppose we should pray for these people, as they are three percent of the world's population. I am deeply scarred forever by what she did, as she committed an act of mental suicide to me and my loving parents....but she will never know she is, because she is, and always will be, a devout sociopath."

72

BLOG EXCHANGES: LOST CHILDREN

THE REST OF US CANNOT understand the mind of a sociopath, not their influence, because we cannot imagine using manipulation to the point of damaging someone else's well-being; we cannot imagine hurting someone just because they "rejected" us. It's not healthy for a child of any age to be completely cut off from a parent. Yet sociopaths heartlessly decide to keep children away from the other parent, if that other parent leaves. To fight sociopathy is to reach into a dark void, hoping for just one shred of human empathy, and to come back with nothing because there is nothing humane on the other side.

L: One thought on what to look for in relationships, in trying to avoid the same pain for our children, is spotting the DRAMA. There will always be relationship drama EARLY in those boyfriends (or girlfriends). The fights are gut wrenching for the healthier of the two and common for the sick one. That's a part of controlling everything from situations... to emotions... but healthy people don't recognize it; just like someone speaking a completely foreign language can be saying something really awful and we don't even have a concept of the content...so the abuser 'speaks' that foreign language of control and the non-controlling one doesn't 'hear' what's really being said/done.

About the issue of being separated from our children, by the abuser, is a tough one for me. It just hit me last night that I have now been separated from my oldest child's life almost as long as I was allowed to be her mother. Typing these words still cuts through my heart. My chest is hurting as I sit here. She is celebrating her 26 birthday on the 12th of this Christmas month but moved out of my house when she was 14 and into the toxic home of my ex and his alcoholic then-wife #2. It's almost too much to bear. I really don't know if I have the answers....still. The children of these unions seem to be a toss-up. The more children of that relationship; the more likely at least one will believe the lies. Is is genetic? Could it be that child is more like the abuser? Will they ever come to some understanding of both sides? When we look at the horrible truth that the abuser never seems to 'get it' we then have to look at the gut wrenching possibility that our very flesh and blood child-that we adore and would die for- may never get it either. I am now 12 years into this almost total alienation from my firstborn daughter's life. As a married adult, she has somehow shut out this entire part of her family, baby sister, grandparents and even full sister at times. I don't get it and maybe never will. I have to pray for her and love her from a distance."

73 LIFE ON THE OTHER SIDE

IN SEPTEMBER 2013, I POSTED this to my blog:

"A lot has happened this past summer. To move in with Steven was the best decision I could've made for my son and me. Often I think that God put Steven in my life even more for my son then for me. Physical health is obviously interrelated to emotional and mental health. He has gained nineteen pounds and grown four inches. He doesn't have any digestive issues anymore. He eats whatever we cook and is an overall well behaved, adjusted and healthy boy. He loves his new school and is thriving. He went from being one of the smallest boys in his class at school to being one of the biggest. He is strong, confident, speaks up for himself, popular (we have kids running through our house whenever we allow it)—he smiles all the time. I love being his mom and tell him every day.

Today, we have had a typical peaceful Sunday. I've sat on the porch working and watching Steven close our pool. He works so hard around the house. Peter's idea of working outside of the house was proudly trimming the shrubs leaving the scraps for me to gather, which is a good picture of our union. I do not take Steven for granted and am thankful for everything he does. And my gratefulness is reciprocated; I am thanked and loved tenderly, daily. My work productivity has increased exponentially.

Now, a group of neighborhood boys have congregated on our back porch to watch Steven practice shooting his compound bow, from now sixty yards. He is the Super Hero of the neighborhood.

I can't wait to spend every day with Steven—a team working side by side. In these past few months, we have had our struggles but that doesn't stop him from being loving, patient and kind. He looks at me as if he's seeing me for the first time every day—so lovingly. He tells me constantly I am smart and beautiful—the smartest, most beautiful woman he's ever known. He tells me I am his soul mate and life partner. He validates me, encourages me, helps me, is proud of the littlest things, and forgives me without reserve or reminder. He loves my son easily and gives without request; he is a great dad. I know unconditional love now. I never thought this even existed. And of course his sentiments are reciprocated with the same intensity and sincerity. We have a mutual and unbreakable bond. We've gone through the worst. It's time for us to embrace our experiences and our callings, enjoy each moment and each other. I believe in happily ever after.

. . . . .

The year to follow, September 2013 through September 2014 was the worst year in either Steven's or my life. Peter and Jo weren't done with us; they launched a campaign that succeeded in damaging us, psychologically, mentally, spiritually and financially. They would not, could not, leave us alone. We had dared to divorce socio-paths… The worst was yet to come.

Acknowledgments

I would first like to thank my parents for their immediate and ongoing unconditional love and support and helping me financially, when I faced losing my son. My attorney, Robin S., who fiercely defended me, working my case pro-bono at times. My therapist, who helped me navigate through the courts and helped me function from day to day. Thank you to all of my friends, who stand out during this time in my life: Laura S., Cathy B., Lynn B., Laverne B., Janet, Stephanie, Laura B., Marla, Beth, Peg, Linda, Sarah, Deb, Karen, Tina, Sue, Jerri, Jeff J., Jeff K., Doug, J., J.M., Lisa, Carolyn, Angie, Danyelle, Jac, Kara, Nicole, Val, neighbors, church friends, and therapy group friends, all who spent hours listening and supporting. I'd like to thank Sue Black for being a great support to me while she was a research assistant and then text editing this book. Thank you to 529 books for their beautiful cover and design work.

About the Author

Sabrina Brown is an Associate Professor of Epidemiology at the University of Kentucky. She received her Master of Public Health and Doctor of Public Health there. Sabrina has three children; two daughters, age 26 and 23, and a son, 13, who lives solely with her and her husband Steven Brown, whom she married in 2013.

References

1. Bandura A. Self-efficacy: toward a unifying theory of behavioral change. *Psychological Review*, 1977, Vol. 84, No.2, 191-215.

2. Wing CS. Story of the engine that thought it could. *The New York Tribune*, 1906.

3. American Psychological Association. The effects of trauma do not have to last a lifetime. *Psychological Science*. 2017. Viewed 2/2/17 at http://www.apa.org/research/action/ptsd.aspx.

4. Evans PE. The verbally abusive relationship: how to recognize it and how to respond. *Adams Media*, 2010.

5. Bach GR, Deutsch R. Stop! You're driving me crazy. *New York; G.P. Putnam's Sons*, 1980; p.16.

6. Stout M. The sociopath next door: the ruthless versus the rest of us. *Three River Press*, 2005.

7. Lenzenweger MF, Lane MC, Loranger AW, Kessler RC (2007). DSM-IV personality disorders in the National Comorbidity Survey Replication. *Biological Psychiatry*, 2007; 62(6), 553-564.

8. American Psychiatric Association's Diagnostic and Statistical Manual of Mental Disorders, fifth edition (DSM-V). 2012. Viewed 2/2/17 at http://www.psi.uba.ar/academica/car-

rerasdegrado/psicologia/sitios_catedras/practicas_profe-sionales/820_clinica_tr_personalidad_psicosis/mate-rial/dsm.pdf.

9. List of Human Emotions. Viewed 2/2/17 at http://www.listof-humanemotions.com/disgust

10. Larsson S. The girl with the dragon tattoo. *Vintage Crime/Black Lizard, Vintage Books,* 2009; p 449-450.

11. Rivera EA, Zeoli AM, Sullivan CM. Abused mothers' safety concerns and court mediators' custody recommendations. *J Fam Violence.* 2012; 27(4): 321–332.

12. Excerpted from: Gardner, R.A.. The parental alienation syndrome, second edition. *Creative Therapeutics*, Inc, 1998.

13. Drugs.com. Know more. Be sure. Antabuse. Viewed 3/12/17 at https://www.drugs.com/antabuse.html.

14. Liem EB, Joiner TV, Tsueda K, Sessler DI. Increased sensitivity to thermal pain and reduced subcutaneous lidocaine efficacy in redheads. *Anesthesiology.* 2005; 102(3): 509-514.

15. The Alabama Coalition Against Domestic Violence. Escape this site. Viewed 2/2/17 at http://www.acadv.org/abus-ers.html.

16. Adkins, K.S., Dush, C.M.Kamp. The mental health of mothers in and after violent and controlling unions. *Social Science Research.* 39 (2010) 925-937.

I MARRIED A SOCIOPATH